Insight VCE Revision Questions

Media Units 3 & 4

First published in 2024
Insight Publications Pty Ltd
3/350 Charman Road
Cheltenham Victoria 3192
Australia

Tel: +61 3 8571 4950
Email: books@insightpublications.com.au

www.insightpublications.com.au

Insight VCE Revision Questions: Media Units 3 & 4

ISBN: 9781923154988

Written and reviewed by Rachael Swatman and Ellie Katsaouni
Cover by Melisa Paredes
Internal design by Bec Yule @ Red Chilli Design
Layout by Ana Maria Sastre
Edited by Carole Lander
Proofread by Sage Napthine-Morrison
Printed by Markono Print Media Pte Ltd

Insight Publications acknowledges the Traditional Custodians of the Country on which we meet and work, the Boonwurrung People of the Kulin Nation. We pay our respects to their Elders past and present, and extend that respect to all Aboriginal and Torres Strait Islander peoples.

Contents

Introduction

This *VCE Revision Questions: Media Units 3 & 4* resource contains questions, suggested responses and tips to help you develop skills for assessment. We recommend using this resource as part of your study regime by completing sets of questions, as this process of applying your understanding and actively recalling information assists with deeper learning. You will also be able to review your answers and assess their appropriateness and correctness against the provided sample responses. Note that this resource complies with the 2024–2028 VCE Media Study Design.

In this resource, you will find exam-style questions and high-level sample responses covering each area of study in the Study Design for Units 3 and 4. According to the VCAA Exam Specifications, the Media exam will have a Section A and Section B, and any of these areas of study may be examined in Section A of the exam. However, questions in Section B may cover Unit 3, Area of Study 1 and Unit 4, Area of Study 2. Consequently, both the Section A and Section B styles of questions are provided for each of these areas of study.

By using *VCE Revision Questions: Media Units 3 & 4* as part of your study regime throughout the year, you will be prepared for questions you may encounter in your end-of-year VCE examination.

We wish you well with your studies.

The Insight Team

Questions

Unit 3 | Area of Study 1 Narratives and their contexts Section A

Question 1 (3 marks)

Explain how the construction of a media form can shape media narratives and how audiences engage with them.

Question 2 (4 marks)

Explain how media codes and/or conventions influence how an audience engages with, consumes or reads media narratives.

Question 3 (7 marks)

Discuss the relationship between media narratives and their contexts of production. In your response, refer to a media narrative that you have studied this year.

Selected media narrative: ______________________

Question 4 (5 marks)

Describe how **one** of the codes or conventions used in a media narrative you studied this year was used to convey meaning in **one** scene or section of this narrative.

Selected media narrative: ____________________

Question 5 (4 marks)

Discuss a way in which the intended audience of a media narrative you studied this year may have engaged with, consumed or read the product differently to an audience from a different context.

Selected media narrative: ____________________

Question 6 (6 marks)

a. Explain how an audience from a specific context engaged with, consumed or read a media narrative that you have studied this year. 3 marks

Selected media narrative:

b. Explain how an audience from a different context engaged with, consumed or read the same media narrative. 3 marks

Question 7 (4 marks)

Analyse how **one** code and **one** convention worked in conjunction to convey meaning in a media narrative that you have studied this year.

Selected media narrative: ______________________

Question 8 (3 marks)

Explain how the construction of a media narrative can reflect the media form in which it is produced.

Question 9 (3 marks)

Explain **one** feature of construction within a media form that you have studied this year.

Selected media form:

Question 10 (7 marks)

Discuss the relationship that a media narrative that you have studied this year may have had with audiences from **two** different contexts and how they may have read, consumed or engaged with that media narrative.

Selected media narrative:

Question 11 (6 marks)

Analyse how meaning conveyed through codes and/or conventions may have influenced audience engagement in **one** media narrative that you have studied this year.

Selected media narrative:

Question 12 (3 marks)

Explain how **one** characteristic of a media form was evident in the construction of a media narrative that you have studied this year.

Selected media narrative:

Question 13 (7 marks)

Analyse how a media narrative that you have studied this year constructs representations and how they reflect or challenge views and values of their context.

Selected media narrative:

Question 14 (6 marks)

Discuss the ways in which the intended audience may have engaged with, consumed or read a media narrative differently to an audience from a different context. In your response, refer to a media narrative that you have studied this year.

Selected media narrative: ______________________

Question 15 (6 marks)

Discuss how a media narrative that you have studied this year may be read by audiences from different contexts.

Selected media narrative: ______________________

Question 16 (6 marks)

Analyse how **one** media code and **one** media convention work together to convey meaning in a media narrative that you have studied this year.

Selected media narrative: ______________________

Unit 3 | Area of Study 1 Narratives and their contexts Section B

Question 1 (15 marks)

Within the media industry, practitioners rely on a series of technical and symbolic codes and established narrative conventions to convey meaning to their audiences.

Referring to the media narrative that you have studied this year, analyse how ideas have been constructed and/or represented through codes and conventions.

Question 2 (15 marks)

Discuss how the relationship between media narratives and their audiences is reflected in at least one of the following:

- production
- distribution
- consumption
- reception.

In your response, refer to the media narrative you have studied this year.

Question 3 (15 marks)

Analyse the way the context in which an audience consumes a media narrative may impact their engagement with, and/or their reading of, the narrative.

In your response, refer to the media narrative that you have studied this year, and the way it was shaped by the contexts in which it was produced or read, such as the social, historical, institutional, cultural, economic and/or political contexts.

Question 4 (15 marks)

Discuss how media codes and conventions were able to convey meaning to an audience in the media narrative that you have studied this year.

In your response, refer to at least two of the following: social, historical, institutional, cultural, economic and political contexts.

Unit 3 | Area of Study 2 Research, development and experimentation

Question 1 (4 marks)

Outline how you used an idea or technique that has been developed by another creator in your own production.

Question 2 (5 marks)

a. Identify the media form you explored in your pre-production. 1 mark

Selected media form:

b. Explain how your research or investigation of this media form and existing media products shaped the planning of your production and the narrative you wanted to tell. 4 marks

Question 3 (2 marks)

Identify **two** steps you took to develop **one** idea for your media product.

Question 4 (4 marks)

Discuss how **one** of your production experiments helped refine or develop your skills in your selected media form.

Question 5 (4 marks)

Explain how research into your media form's genre and/or style helped to develop your proposed production.

Question 6 (5 marks)

Discuss how a media practitioner you researched used a code or convention to create meaning, and how this influenced your production.

Question 7 (3 marks)

Explain how a skill you developed in the research, development and experimentation stage was appropriate to **either** your selected media form **or** your proposed media product.

Question 8 (3 marks)

Explain why experimentation with equipment, media technologies, and processes is important in the production of a media product.

Question 9 (3 marks)

a. Identify **one** example of media equipment. 1 mark

b. Identify **one** example of a media technology. 1 mark

c. Identify **one** example of a media process. 1 mark

Question 10 (4 marks)

Discuss how your research into your chosen media form and products helped you to identify a skill you wanted to develop or refine for your media product.

Question 11 (3 marks)

How did your production experiments help you to communicate your genre or style to your intended audience?

Question 12 (4 marks)

Outline what your research revealed about the way audiences are engaged by the structural and/or aesthetic qualities of media products, with reference to **two** specific examples.

Question 13 (3 marks)

Explain how **one** component of your research informed the development of your skills in your selected media form.

Selected media form:

Question 14 (5 marks)

Identify **one** process you used to document the development of a media product and discuss how this helped you to realise and/or resolve your pre-production plan.

Question 15 (5 marks)

Explain how you were able to develop **one** skill in the use of media equipment, technologies or processes specific to your selected media form during your research, development and experimentation stage.

Unit 3 | Area of Study 3 Pre-production planning

Question 1 (4 marks)

Outline **two** elements of the production process that you had to consider when constructing your production timeline.

Question 2 (5 marks)

Outline the primary intention of your media product, and explain the specific ways you designed your product to ensure you were able to achieve this.

Question 3 (4 marks)

Discuss how you developed written and visual planning documents for your media product in your pre-production plan, and how this enabled you to plan your product.

Question 4 (6 marks)

Identify **two** media codes or conventions embedded in your media product, and discuss how these were relevant to your selected form, product and/or audience.

Question 5 (3 marks)

Discuss **one** media process you undertook to develop your proposed narrative.

Question 6 (5 marks)

Discuss how you intended to use **one** code and/or convention to engage your audience with your media product.

Unit **4** | Area of Study **1** Media production

Question 1 (5 marks)

Discuss how **one** code and **one** convention that you applied in your pre-production plan were appropriate to your selected narrative.

Question 2 (6 marks)

Media creators and producers work with others and reflect in order to gain insight into whether their products communicate their planned intent.

Discuss the impact your feedback and reflection processes had on your final product with reference to **two** specific examples.

Question 3 (3 marks)

Explain how a written or visual document you created has impacted your production plan.

Question 4 (3 marks)

Describe how the intended audience outlined in your pre-production plan is reflected in your media product.

Question 5 (4 marks)

Discuss how you applied production processes appropriate to **either** your media form **or** your media narrative in your pre-production plan.

Question 6 (5 marks)

Explain how **one** key refinement you made between pre-production and the completion of your media product helped you to achieve your intention for your media product.

Question 7 (5 marks)

Discuss **two** factors that led to the refinement of materials, technologies and/or processes used in your production.

Question 8 (5 marks)

Evaluate how effectively your reflection or feedback process during media production enabled you to refine and resolve your media product.

Unit 4 | Area of Study 2 Agency and control in the media Section A

Question 1 (3 marks)

Explain **one** way in which globalisation has impacted how Australian audiences consume media products.

Question 2 (5 marks)

Analyse the way the contemporary media landscape challenges the traditional theories used by academics and commentators to explain the nature of communication between the media and its audience.

Question 3 (6 marks)

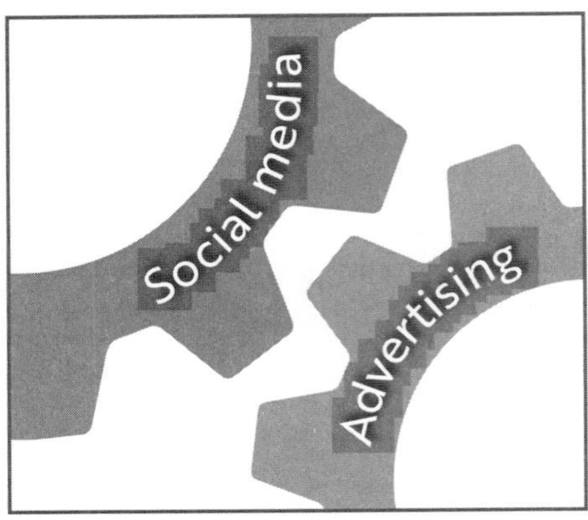

Source: Alex Hariyandi / Shutterstock.com

Discuss how the image above reflects ethical or legal issues in the production, distribution, consumption and/or reception of media products.

Question 4 (4 marks)

Describe **one** ethical or legal issue that relates to the production, distribution, consumption and/or reception of user-generated content.

Question 5 (6 marks)

Source: lukeruk/Shutterstock.com

Source: Atstock Productions / Shutterstock.com

The images above show two ways advertising can appear in the media: one in a more traditional form and one in a more contemporary form.

Discuss how these images demonstrate the way commercial content has evolved over time. In your response, refer to the legal and/or ethical issues that can arise as a result of these changes.

Question 6 (5 marks)

Analyse how **one** globalised media institution or individual has attempted to use the media to exert control over an audience.

Question 7 (5 marks)

Discuss **one** challenge facing Australia's regulatory bodies that has arisen from their inability to control the content that individuals can access in the contemporary globalised media landscape.

Question 8 (4 marks)

Explain the issues and challenges that arise in attempts to regulate and control the media, with reference to a specific example.

Question 9 (5 marks)

How has the harvesting and sale of personal information created an ethical and/or legal issue in the media? In your response, refer to at least **two** of the following:

- the production of media products
- the distribution of media products
- the consumption of media products
- the reception of media products.

Question 10 (5 marks)

a. Identify an issue or challenge relating to regulation and control of the media. 1 mark

b. Explain why your answer to **part a.** presents an issue or challenge for the regulation and control of the media. In your response, refer to how media platforms or regulatory bodies manage or regulate the media. 4 marks

Question 11 (6 marks)

Explain **two** ways the relationship between the media and its audience has changed over time.

Question 12 (4 marks)

Describe **one** instance in which the media was thought to have exerted influence over audiences.

Question 13 (6 marks)

How is the changing relationship between the media and audiences reflected in individuals' use of the media?

Question 14 (5 marks)

As the media increasingly crosses national borders, governments struggle to maintain control over the laws and policies created for their jurisdictions.

Source: The VCE Media Study Design © Victorian Curriculum and Assessment Authority (VCAA), reproduced by permission

Discuss **one** issue that has challenged the Australian Government's ability to manage or regulate media use.

Question 15 (3 marks)

Explain how **both** the media and audiences may exercise agency.

Question 16 (4 marks)

Discuss **one** example that reflects the way the relationship between audiences and global media institutions has changed over time.

Question 17 (7 marks)

Analyse how **one** ethical or legal issue can be seen in the production and/or distribution of media products.

Question 18 (3 marks)

Explain why regulating or controlling the media can be challenging.

Question 19 (7 marks)

Source: eamesBot/Shutterstock.com

Evaluate **either** one ethical **or** one legal issue that can arise in the production, distribution, consumption or reception of media products. You **must** refer to the image in your response.

Question 20 (6 marks)

'No two generations will experience the media in the same way.'

Analyse the ways in which the relationship between the media and audiences is constantly changing.

Unit 4 | Area of Study 2 Agency and control in the media Section B

Question 1 (15 marks)

The relationship between the media and its audience is frequently changing. This is evidenced by the development of new modes of production, distribution, consumption and reception through the creation of social networking platforms.

Discuss the way media influence and audience agency has changed over time. In your response, refer to the issues and challenges relating to regulation and control over the media.

Question 2 (15 marks)

There is a dynamic and changing relationship between the media and audiences.

Discuss at least **two** theories about the influence of both the media and audiences. In your response, refer to how the relationship between the media and audiences has changed over time.

Question 3 (15 marks)

In the modern media landscape, it is commonly accepted that the media and its audiences each have the capacity to influence the other.

Discuss the extent to which the media and its audiences are able to exercise agency.

Question 4 (15 marks)

Evaluate the impact of **one** legal or ethical issue that has arisen in the media landscape. In your response, refer to **at least two** of the following:

- the production of media products
- the distribution of media products
- the consumption of media products
- the reception of media products.

Question 5 (15 marks)

The media landscape is becoming increasingly difficult to regulate and control, due largely to the frequently changing relationship between the media and its audience.

Analyse **two** issues or challenges faced in the regulation and control of the media.

Question 6 (15 marks)

Analyse how both the media and audiences influence the modern media landscape. In your response, refer to how the media is used by **two** of the following:

- globalised media institutions
- individuals
- governments
- audiences.

Sample responses

Unit 3 | Area of Study 1 Narratives and their contexts Section A

Question 1

Sample response

> Media narratives in television are constructed to reflect the specific requirements of this media form. One example is the choice to include a segment at the beginning of each episode catching viewers up on what has happened previously. In the traditional format, episodes of television programs were spaced at daily or weekly intervals, meaning it was more likely that audiences might miss an episode or need a refresher on what occurred in the last episode. During this time, 'previously on' segments offered an important summary of crucial information. These days, with the advent of streaming platforms such as Netflix, audience engagement has changed and they are less likely to need these reminders. Streaming has enabled audiences to catch up on missed episodes easily, and they are more likely to be consuming a show in a 'binge' fashion, negating the need for 'previously on' segments.

Note: This response discusses 'previously on' segments. Other examples from film and television include the traditional Hollywood three-act structure, the use of canned laughter, and changes made to a story's narrative to suit the platform on which it is viewed.

Mark allocation: 3 marks

- 3 marks: The student has provided a clear and accurate overview of how a correctly identified characteristic or element of construction contributes specifically to a media form. They may have supported this assertion with an example.
- 2 marks: The student has correctly identified a characteristic or element of construction. They have provided a limited overview of how it contributes to a media form, and may not have used an example to support their assertion.
- 1 mark: The student has correctly identified a characteristic or element of construction of the media form they studied.

Question 2

Sample response

Media codes and conventions form a significant part of audience reading and engagement, as they are encoded with symbolism that is decoded independently by audiences. For instance, in *Moonlight* (Jenkins, 2016), colour is used throughout the film to convey ideas to the audience. The film's mise en scène heavily features the colours white, green and blue, which are incorporated into props and costumes to establish a connection between Chiron (Alex Hibbert) and characters with whom he feels an affinity. In stark contrast, the use of the colours red, pink and purple are seen primarily when Chiron is experiencing distress. When Paula (Naomie Harris) glares at Chiron down the hallway, her red singlet top is bright against the blue walls, with the sharp pink neon light from her room casting a purple shadow behind her. The audience may infer the growing divide between the characters through the symbolic application of colour in the scene.

Mark allocation: 4 marks

- 4 marks: The student has constructed a detailed and sophisticated response that demonstrates an insightful understanding of the relationship between codes and conventions and audiences. The answer is supported with specific evidence, either from one of their studied media narratives or an alternative source, and appropriate media language is used.
- 3 marks: The student has constructed a clear response that demonstrates a sound understanding of the relationship between codes and conventions and audiences. The answer is supported with relevant evidence. Appropriate media language is used in the response.
- 2 marks: The student has constructed a response that demonstrates a basic understanding of the relationship between codes and conventions and audiences. The student may have incorporated some basic supporting evidence. Some use of appropriate media language is evident in the response.
- 1 mark: The student has constructed a limited response that addresses some part of the question but may be incomplete. The student may simply have identified the media codes and/or conventions and made a broad statement about their effect. The response contains little or no use of appropriate media language.

TIPS

- » **This question gives the opportunity for, but does not require, you to refer specifically to a narrative you studied in class this year.**
- » **It is important to use appropriate media language in your responses. For this question, relevant media language may relate to codes and conventions (e.g. camera techniques, point of view, parallel editing etc.) or discussion of audience (e.g. reception, consumption, engagement or narrative possibilities).**

Question 3

Sample response

Selected media narrative: *Get Out* (2017)

Media creators both explicitly and implicitly reflect the contexts in which their narratives are produced. Their products are embedded with meaning that reflects the creators' ideas and the choices made throughout the production process. Media narratives may explicitly support the dominant views and values of the societies in which they are created, such as by using character dialogue to espouse particular beliefs or by constructing particular representations of groups of people within that society. However, the worldviews of media creators may also more subtly shape the narratives they create. For example, a creator may implicitly reject an ideological view or value such as feminism by portraying women in traditional gender roles, denying them dialogue or relying on tropes such as the damsel in distress or the femme fatale.

The ending of Jordan Peele's 2017 horror film *Get Out* was specifically constructed to reflect the cultural and political context of the film's production period. In an interview with Oprah Winfrey, Peele asserted that 'the climate that [he] wrote the movie in was the Obama era and the movie was meant to address this post-racial lie – the idea that we're past racism'. This acknowledgement of liberalist values in modern American society serves to exemplify the impact of social context on media narratives. Initially, Peele planned to end the film with Chris (Daniel Kaluuya) in prison for the murder of the Armitage family; however, Peele recognised that, by the time the film was ready for release, the Black Lives Matter movement and the political success of Donald Trump meant that audiences 'needed a hero'. The cinematic release thus ends with Chris being picked up by his friend Rod (Lil Rel Howery), and the two escape unscathed. The delayed reveal that it is Rod in the police car that pulls up, however, serves to build tension in an audience who is likely to be familiar with the Black Lives Matter movement, and as Chris raises his hands dejectedly, he represents African Americans such as Philando Castile, Alton Sterling and Michael Brown Jr, who were fatally shot by police officers. His visible relief when Rod says his name is thus likely to be mirrored by Peele's intended audience. Peele responded to a perceived political and cultural shift in American society by choosing to forgo the 'dose of sobering reality' he initially wanted to serve to those who held the belief that America was no longer prone to racism due to their election of a Black president. Instead he offered a means of 'escapism' to those engaged in the ongoing fight against discrimination, who actively push progressive values through protests, rallies and social media discourse.

Note: This sample response is of a higher level than a typical student response, in order to show the range of detail that can be used to answer the question.

Mark allocation: 7 marks

- 6–7 marks: The student has constructed a comprehensive analysis of the relationship between media narratives and the social, historical, institutional, cultural, economic and political contexts in which they are produced. Specific and detailed examples from the selected media narrative have been provided, and the student has conveyed strong insight into how specific aspects of the context of the narrative's production period are reflected in the product. Appropriate media language has been effectively used throughout the response.
- 4–5 marks: The student has constructed a clear analysis of the relationship between media narratives and the social, historical, institutional, cultural, economic and political contexts in which they are produced. Relevant examples from the selected media narrative have been provided, and the student has conveyed insight into how aspects of the context of the narrative's production period are reflected in the product. The student has used appropriate media language throughout their response.
- 2–3 marks: The student has constructed a general analysis of the relationship between media narratives and the social, historical, institutional, cultural, economic and political contexts in which they are produced. Examples from the selected media narrative may have been provided, but these may be broad or less relevant. The student has conveyed some insight into how the context of the narrative's production period is reflected in the product, and some media language has been used.
- 1 mark: The student has provided a limited or incomplete response that has made some attempt to answer the question.

TIPS

» **A useful approach to a question such as this one is to begin your response by analysing the relationship between narratives and their contexts more generally, before incorporating examples to support your argument.**

» **You are welcome to include the year of the release of a media narrative in your response if you wish, though you are not required to do so unless there are two versions of the media narrative with the same name.**

Question 4

Sample response

Selected media narrative: *Whiplash*

In the opening sequence of his 2014 film *Whiplash*, Damien Chazelle uses editing as a technique to foreshadow the narrative arc and eventual unravelling of protagonist Neiman (Miles Teller). Chazelle layers the title over a black screen with the non-diegetic sound of a drum beat that begins slowly, gradually building to a frenzy. As the drumming reaches its climax, Chazelle cuts dramatically from black to a long shot of a hallway, drawing a connection between the concept of whiplash (an injury caused by a sudden acceleration or deceleration). At the end of the hallway, we see Neiman sitting at a drum kit under a spotlight, conveying the idea that the primary focus of this narrative is the relationship Neiman has with his art, and foreshadowing that the building pressure of the narrative will impact him directly.

Mark allocation: 5 marks

- 4–5 marks: The student has provided a detailed and insightful example of how the selected code or convention has been used to convey meaning in one scene or section of one media narrative. Effective media language is used in the response.
- 3 marks: The student has provided a clear and relevant example of how the selected code or convention has been used to convey meaning in one scene or section of one media narrative. Relevant media language is used in the response.
- 2 marks: The student has provided a general example of how the selected code or convention has been used to convey meaning in one scene or section of one media narrative. Some media language is used in the response.
- 1 mark: The student has provided a weak example of how the selected code or convention has been used to convey meaning in one scene or section of one media narrative. The student may not have referred specifically to one scene or section, and may have talked about the narrative as a whole. Limited or no media language is used in the response.

Question 5

Sample response

Selected media narrative: *Children of Men*

Alfonso Cuarón's 2006 film *Children of Men* may provoke vastly disparate reactions from its audiences in different contexts. For example, in a present-day context, the audience would react very differently compared to the intended audience at the time of its release. The film was released to UK audiences in September 2006, just over a year after the July 2005 London bombings. The attack occurred just one day after London won its bid to host the 2012 Olympics. Both of these events are referenced in the film and may have prompted a deeply emotional response from audiences viewing the narrative, due to temporal proximity. In the opening sequence, Theo (Clive Owen) leaves a coffee shop and walks out onto a dirty, dystopian street – recognisable as London due to Cuarón's inclusion of the city's red double-decker buses – only for the cafe to blow up moments after his departure. The early morning timing of the explosion and its central London location may have affected audiences who had experienced a similar event in their home country recently, indicating how political and social contexts can affect how audiences engage with a product.

Mark allocation: 4 marks

- 4 marks: The student has provided a sophisticated discussion of the way in which audiences from different contexts engage with, consume or read media narratives. A highly relevant idea has been identified and described in detail. A specific and highly appropriate example from the media narrative has been used to substantiate discussion. Effective application of media language is evident in the response.
- 3 marks: The student has provided a detailed discussion of a way in which audiences from different contexts engage with, consume or read media narratives. Appropriate ideas have been identified and described in detail. A specific and relevant example from a media narrative has been used to substantiate discussion. Thorough use of appropriate media language is evident in the response.
- 2 marks: The student has provided a general discussion of the ways in which audiences from different contexts engage with, consume or read media narratives. An idea has been generally identified and described. A basic example from a media narrative has been used to substantiate discussion. Some application of media language is evident in the response.
- 1 mark: The student has provided a limited discussion of a way in which audiences from different contexts engage with, consume or read media narratives. An idea has been identified but not described. Limited or general references to a media narrative have been used as part of the response. An attempt to use media language is evident; however, this is mostly irrelevant or incorrect.

Question 6a.

Sample response

Selected media narrative: *Baby Driver*

When the film *Baby Driver* (2017, Wright) was initially released to American audiences in June 2017, fans of Edgar Wright were eagerly anticipating the director's newest offering. This was in part due to its all-star casting line-up. Early commentary particularly focused on the director's choice to cast Ansel Elgort, Jon Hamm, Jamie Foxx and Kevin Spacey in significant roles, suggesting that the multi-award-winning cast would bring a high calibre of acting to the film and draw a large audience to the box office. This expectation was confirmed when the film earned $226.9 million at the box office, suggesting that the intended audiences were responding positively to the film's premise and casting.

Mark allocation: 3 marks

- 3 marks: A thoughtful response that demonstrates detailed understanding of how a specific audience's context may have affected its engagement, consumption or reading of a specific narrative. Relevant media language is used in the response.
- 2 marks: A general response that demonstrates clear understanding of how a specific audience's context may have affected its engagement, consumption or reading of a specific narrative. Some media language is used in the response.
- 1 mark: A limited response that demonstrates a basic understanding of how an audience's context may have affected its engagement, consumption or reading of a specific narrative. An audience from a specific context has been correctly identified. Limited or no media language is used in the response.

Note: If the student answers with a broad demographic, for example, 'children' or 'millennials', they cannot receive a mark.

TIP

» **Make sure you clearly define your audience and the context.**

Question 6b.

Sample response

> A global audience viewing *Baby Driver* in 2024 may respond less positively to the film's storyline and characterisations due to the allegations made about Kevin Spacey in 2017 at the height of the #MeToo movement. In October 2017, actor Anthony Rapp alleged that Spacey had made sexual advances towards him when Rapp was 14. Further allegations then came out that saw Spacey arraigned on criminal charges for the assault of other young men. This contextual factor may affect the way a modern audience engages with the film, especially given Spacey's character, Doc, displays a somewhat inappropriate and predatory fixation with Elgort's Baby throughout the film. Thus, the dynamic between the characters may be heightened by the actors' contexts. Multiple articles have been penned suggesting that *Baby Driver* is now 'unwatchable' and 'unbearably creepy'.

Mark allocation: 3 marks

- Marks are allocated according to the same criteria as **part a.** If the student has referenced a different narrative to **part a.**, no marks can be awarded.

Question 7

Sample response

Selected media narrative: *1917*

In *1917* (Mendes, 2019), the technical code of editing was used in conjunction with the convention of structure of time in order to convey the direct experience of Lance Corporal William Schofield as he struggles to achieve his mission. Mendes employs the use of editing techniques in order to give the impression that the entire film consists of a single, uninterrupted shot. The structure of time is linear and limited to the direct experience of Schofield, a technique that aims to convey his constant awareness of his dawn deadline. In the film's narrative, Schofield passes out, represented by a cut to black that holds for a number of seconds. When Schofield awakens, hours have passed, with his lapse in consciousness being conveyed through the compression of a significant amount of time into seconds. In this way, Mendes employs editing and structure of time in conjunction in order to engage the audience in Schofield's plight, creating a deeply personal connection between audience and character, and heightening the tension of the seemingly impossible deadline the protagonist is trying to meet.

Mark allocation: 4 marks

- 4 marks: The student has provided a clear and relevant example of how one code and one convention are used to convey meaning in a media narrative. They have articulated a competent understanding of how the selected code and convention work in conjunction. Effective media language is used in the response.
- 3 marks: The student has provided a general example of how one code and one convention are used to convey meaning in a media narrative. They have an articulated an appropriate understanding of how the selected code and convention work in conjunction. Relevant media language is used in the response.
- 2 marks: The student has provided an example of how one code and one convention are used to convey meaning in a media narrative. They have articulated some understanding of how codes and conventions can be used in conjunction. Some media language is used in the response.
- 1 mark: The student has provided a limited example of how one code and one convention are used to convey meaning in a media narrative. They may not have addressed how the code and convention work in conjunction. Limited or no media language is used in the response.

Question 8

Sample response

> A primary difference between television and film narratives is that television storylines are often constructed episodically, with the story often reaching a cliffhanger moment towards the end of an episode in order to encourage the audience to watch the next one. However, the construction of a film narrative often reflects the one-off nature of the story, and as such the three-act plot structure has become a key component of traditional Hollywood films.

Mark allocation: 3 marks

- 3 marks: A considered response that demonstrates a detailed understanding of how the form in which a media product is made affects the construction of the media narrative. Relevant media language is used in the response.
- 2 marks: A general response that demonstrates a clear understanding of how the form in which a media product is made affects the construction of the media narrative. Some media language is used in the response.
- 1 mark: A limited response that demonstrates a basic understanding of how the form in which a media product is made affects the construction of the media narrative. Limited or no media language is used in the response.

Question 9

Sample response

> Selected media form: episodic arc structure
>
> Episodic arc structure is a feature of construction within the media form of television. Due to television shows running in seasons, which are made up of a number of episodes, the structure within an episode does not need to adhere to traditional Hollywood story arcs, but rather needs to work in conjunction with the other episodes in the season, or even the final episode of the preceding season or the first episode of the following season. This may mean that interruptions to the protagonist's stasis may not be resolved in a single episode – instead, the episode will develop an element of the central conflict and most likely establish further complications to draw the viewer into the following episode.

Mark allocation: 3 marks

- 3 marks: A thoughtful response that demonstrates a detailed understanding of how one construction element features within the selected media form. Relevant media language is used in the response.
- 2 marks: A general response that demonstrates a clear understanding of how one construction element features within the selected media form. Some media language is used in the response.
- 1 mark: A limited response that attempts to identify a feature of construction within a media form, but may not provide additional explanation, or may attempt to explain an incorrect feature of construction.

Question 10

Sample response

Selected media narrative: *Memento*

Audiences from disparate contexts may receive the same media narrative in very different ways. The relationship that Christopher Nolan's film *Memento* (2000) may have had with audiences from the time of its initial release would likely differ greatly to the relationship it would have with a modern audience and context. One significant factor in this relationship is Nolan himself and his reputation as a director. *Memento* is a complicated film that requires audiences to keep track of two different timelines as it communicates ideas about the fallibility of memory. When the film was released, Nolan was virtually unknown and yet to develop the reputation he holds in 2024 for being a blockbuster director who often plays with time structure. A modern audience consuming *Memento* may well bring this knowledge with them and engage more directly with the film's complicated temporal order as a result. In Roger Ebert's 2001 review of *Memento,* he suggested that 'Leonard is adrift in time and experience, and therefore so are we'. This feeling of being adrift in a Nolan film has come to be expected by modern audiences who may have consumed other key pieces of Nolan's work, such as *Inception*, *Interstellar* and *Tenet*; thus, *Memento* may be received as both less confusing and less groundbreaking to an audience in 2024. Furthermore, the psychological components of *Memento's* plot may take on new meaning for modern audiences. As explored by reviewer Peter Bradshaw in *The Guardian* in 2000, the psychological components of *Memento's* plot relating to Leonard's retrograde amnesia felt slightly unbelievable to audiences at the time of release. However, in 2020, Bradshaw revisited the film and suggested that 'dementia has become one of the most urgent issues of our time'. This increasing understanding of those with memory difficulties may enable a modern audience to view Leonard as a more sympathetic character, despite his brutality in the film.

Mark allocation: 7 marks

- 6–7 marks: The student has constructed a comprehensive analysis of the relationship between a media narrative and audiences from two clearly defined contexts. Specific and detailed examples from the media narrative have been provided, and the student has conveyed strong insight into how specific aspects of audience context may impact their relationship with the narrative. The student has used highly appropriate media language throughout their response.
- 4–5 marks: The student has constructed a clear analysis of the relationship between a media narrative and audiences from two different contexts. Relevant examples from the media narrative have been provided, and the student has conveyed insight into how aspects of audience context may impact their relationship with the narrative. The student has used appropriate media language throughout their response.
- 2–3 marks: The student has provided a general discussion of the relationship between a media narrative and audiences from two different contexts. Examples from the media narrative may have been provided, but these may be broad or less relevant, and the student has conveyed some insight into how audience context may impact their relationship with the narrative. The student has used some media language.
- 1 mark: The student has provided a limited or incomplete response that has made some attempt to answer the question.

TIP

» **Take care to clearly signpost the two different contexts in which audiences may have received the media narrative for your examiner (e.g. 'When the film was released …', 'However, in 2024 …').**

Question 11

Sample response

Selected media narrative: *Jojo Rabbit*

In the film *Jojo Rabbit* (2019), director Taika Waititi uses codes and conventions to maintain a balance of comedy and drama in a film with sensitive subject matter. Through acting and sound, Waititi attempts to enable audiences to engage with the humorous components of the film while also recognising the gravely serious nature of the Holocaust. In the scene where Jojo is visited at home by the Gestapo, the phrase 'Heil Hitler' is repeated 31 times in a minute, a script decision that Waititi says was an attempt to 'point out how ridiculous Nazis were'. The joke is taken further when Captain Klenzendorf (Sam Rockwell) asks, 'Did I miss anything?' and Deertz (Stephen Merchant) pleasantly replies, 'No, no, we were just Heil Hitlering the boy, and then Heil Hitlering yourself, and then Heil Hitlering Freddy Finkel and now we are in the midst of a routine inspection'. The overarching purpose of the scene itself is to create tension, which comes from the audience's fear that the inspection may uncover Elsa in Jojo's attic. This drawn-out gag simultaneously provides comedic relief and heightens tension as audiences wait to find out if Elsa will remain safe. Merchant's chilling smile and casual composure convey Deertz to be a dangerous character amid the silliness, as he appears duplicitous and untrustworthy. This focus on both the serious and pathetic aspects of the Gestapo, who are frequently portrayed in media narratives as unquestionably violent and cruel, may have worked to engage audiences by subverting their expectations.

Mark allocation: 6 marks

- 6 marks: A sophisticated analysis of how audience engagement can be influenced by codes and/or conventions in a media narrative. The student has explored how meaning has been conveyed in the narrative and insightfully considered the impact this may have had on audiences. Specific and highly appropriate examples from one media narrative have been used to substantiate discussion. Effective application of media language is evident in the response.
- 5 marks: A detailed analysis of how audience engagement can be influenced by codes and/or conventions in a media narrative. The student has explored how meaning has been conveyed in the narrative and appropriately considered the impact this may have had on audiences. Specific and relevant examples from one media narrative have been used to substantiate discussion. Thorough use of media language is evident in the response.

- 4 marks: A clear analysis of how audience engagement can be influenced by codes and/or conventions in a media narrative. The student has explored how meaning has been conveyed in the narrative and considered the impact this may have had on audiences. Relevant examples from one media narrative have been used to substantiate discussion. Appropriate application of media language is evident in the response.
- 3 marks: A general discussion of how audience engagement can be influenced by codes and/or conventions in a media narrative. The student has explored how meaning has been conveyed in the narrative and broadly considered the impact this may have had on audiences. Basic examples from one media narrative have been used to substantiate discussion. Some application of media language is evident in the response.
- 2 marks: A limited analysis of how audience engagement can be influenced by codes and/or conventions in a media narrative. The student has in some way considered how meaning has been conveyed in the narrative and attempted to link this to an audience's engagement. A general example from one media narrative may have been included. An attempt to use media language is evident in the response.
- 1 mark: An incomplete or very limited response that answers some part of the question. The student may simply have identified one way in which an audience engaged with a narrative or may have identified how codes or conventions have conveyed meaning in the narrative. Little or no use of media language is evident in the response.

TIPS

» **Attempt to pick one scene and analyse it in depth for codes and/or conventions, rather than jumping between scenes and providing a superficial analysis.**

» **Refer to the 'Study specifications' in the Study Design to revise the codes and conventions.**

Question 12

Sample response

Selected media narrative: *30 Rock*

One characteristic in the construction of a television series that is found in *30 Rock* is the use of the cold open or teaser sequence, to establish the premise of its episodes. For instance, the cold open of Season 1, Episode 2 sets up the jealous and competitive dynamic between Tracy and Jenna that will become central to the plot. When Jenna enters the studio, non-diegetic celebrative music starts playing until the band says, 'It's just Jenna'. The camera then cuts to a close-up shot of Jenna's face looking wounded, in conjunction with the abrupt end to the non-diegetic soundtrack. The music then begins again, followed by an eruption of cheers when Tracy enters, his posse blocking Jenna from view until a medium close-up shows her glancing around awkwardly, lips pursed to convey her frustration at the situation.

Mark allocation: 3 marks

- 3 marks: The student has provided a thoughtful response that demonstrates a clear understanding of how one characteristic of a media form can be seen in the construction of the selected media narrative. Relevant media language is used in the response.
- 2 marks: The student has provided a general response that demonstrates a clear understanding of how one characteristic of a media form can be seen in the construction of the selected media narrative. Some media language is used in the response.
- 1 mark: The student has provided a limited response that identifies a characteristic of a media form but may not have provided additional explanation. Limited or no media language is used in the response.

TIP

» **A characteristic relates to the form of your media narrative (e.g. film, television show, photography, print). Characteristics are elements we can expect to find within narratives of a particular form.**

Question 13

Sample response

Selected media narrative: *Kevin Can F**k Himself*

Valerie Armstrong's 2021 dark comedy television series, *Kevin Can F**k Himself*, implicitly comments on the feminist values of its post #MeToo movement context. The series demonstrates how traditional sitcoms encourage and make light of the mistreatment of women. It does this through its dual use of formats: a bright multicamera sitcom interspersed with a dark, cool-toned drama. In the pilot episode, the characters are first introduced in the sitcom format. A middle-class American lounge room is depicted in bright lighting, with a couch central to the shot, reminiscent of shows like *Everybody Loves Raymond* and *The Honeymooners*. As the protagonists – an oafish, overweight slob named Kevin and his exasperated wife, Allison – engage in fast banter with Kevin's idiotic best friend, Neil, the scene displays the kinds of misogynistic jokes typical of sitcoms. An example is when Allison's earnest suggestion that 'Maybe, instead of a rager, we could celebrate our tenth anniversary with something more ... adult' is met with the childish suggestion, 'Like a threesome?' spoken in unison by Kevin and Neil. Kevin is a representation of patriarchal privilege, and the use of the canned laugh track criticises this by reducing Kevin and his friends to caricatures. The alternative drama format is then used to provide a stark contrast to this tone, dramatically drawing attention to the way multicamera sitcoms encourage audiences to find humour in male behaviour that reduces women to a punchline. When Allison exits the lounge room into the kitchen, the comparative diegetic silence as she deflates highlights the effort involved in being married to a man who constantly puts her needs second, and suggests that a traditional, gendered power imbalance in marriage can oppress women. This is paired with a high-pitched ringing that builds until Allison smashes a beer stein on the counter. She examines the blood on her hand, before calling out 'I'm fine' to an imaginary enquiry. In this second format, the facade Allison maintains in the presence of her husband comes down and Armstrong implicitly criticises the value that women are expected to exist in a patriarchal world, suggesting that they must force themselves to put aside their feelings and desires in order to satisfy the men who dominate their lives.

Note: This sample response is of a higher level than a typical student response, in order to show the range of detail that can be used to answer the question.

Mark allocation: 7 marks

- 6–7 marks: The student has constructed a comprehensive analysis of the way representations are constructed and reflect or challenge views and values of a context. Specific and detailed examples from the media narrative have been provided, and the student has conveyed strong insight into how representations can implicitly or explicitly comment on or reject values. The student has used highly appropriate media language throughout their response.
- 4–5 marks: The student has constructed a clear analysis of the way representations are constructed and reflect or challenge views and values of a context. Relevant examples from the media narrative have been provided, and the student has conveyed insight into how representations can implicitly or explicitly comment on or reject values. The student has used appropriate media language throughout their response.

- 2–3 marks: The student has provided a general discussion of the way representations are constructed and reflect or challenge views and values of a context. Examples from the media narrative may have been provided, but these may be broad or less relevant, and the student has conveyed some insight into how representations can implicitly or explicitly comment on or reject values. The student has used some media language throughout their response.
- 1 mark: The student has provided a limited or incomplete response that has made some attempt to answer the question by referencing representations. The student has used limited or no media language in their response.

Question 14

Sample response

Selected media narrative: *Top Gun*

Tony Scott's film *Top Gun* (1986) would have made a very different impact on its first audiences compared to the one it would make on modern audiences. When it was released audiences flocked to cinemas, making it the highest grossing film of that year. The film, which was made with assistance from the US Navy, was seen at the time of its release to have a dramatic impact on Navy recruitment. At some screenings of *Top Gun,* Navy recruitment booths were set up to capitalise on the film's effect and, together with the film's pro-military ideology, this brought about a reported 500 per cent increase in the number of applications to the US Naval aviation forces. In this way, it could be concluded that original audiences engaged with the film in a way that directly reflected its intention.

In contrast, audiences viewing *Top Gun* in a modern setting may respond very differently to the strong pro-military messaging in the film. A Ronald Reagan Institute poll released in March 2021 found that since 2018, there had been a 14 per cent drop in Americans who have 'a great deal of trust and confidence in the military', bringing the total to only 56 per cent. Furthermore, the withdrawal of American troops from Afghanistan in August 2021 and resumption of the Taliban's power started many conversations about the negative impacts and uselessness of war. For this reason, a modern audience may view the story of Lieutenant Pete 'Maverick' Mitchell as being an unrealistic, romanticised representation of war. The film has been criticised in recent years for being far too blatant in its attempts to advertise the military, suggesting modern audiences are not reading the narrative in the same way its original audiences did.

Mark allocation: 6 marks

- 6 marks: The student has provided a sophisticated discussion of the ways in which the intended audience and an audience from a different context may have engaged with, consumed or read a media narrative. The two contexts have been identified and described in detail. Specific and highly appropriate examples relating to one media narrative have been used to substantiate discussion. Effective application of media language is evident in the response.

- 5 marks: The student has provided a detailed discussion of the ways in which the intended audience and an audience from a different context may have engaged with, consumed or read a media narrative. The two contexts have been identified and described in detail. Specific and relevant examples relating to one media narrative have been used to substantiate discussion. Thorough use of appropriate media language is evident in the response.
- 4 marks: The student has provided a clear discussion of the ways in which the intended audience and an audience from a different context may have engaged with, consumed or read a media narrative. The two contexts have been identified and described in general detail. Relevant examples relating to one media narrative have been used to substantiate discussion. Appropriate application of media language is evident in the response.
- 3 marks: The student has provided a general discussion of the ways in which the intended audience and an audience from a different context may have engaged with, consumed or read a media narrative. The two contexts have been generally identified and described. Basic examples relating to one media narrative have been used to substantiate discussion. Some application of media language is evident in the response.
- 2 marks: The student has provided a limited discussion of the ways in which audiences from different contexts may have engaged with, consumed or read a media narrative. At least one context has been identified and described, or two contexts may have been outlined with little or no description. Limited or general references to a media narrative have been used as part of the response. An attempt to use media language is evident; however, this may be with some inaccuracies.
- 1 mark: The student has provided an incomplete or very limited response that answers some part of the question. The student may simply have identified one way in which an audience received a media narrative, or may have discussed a media narrative being received by an audience from a context that is different to the intended audience's context. Little or no use of media language is evident in the response.

TIPS

» **In your response, try to convey a clear understanding of the contextual factors that impact an audience.**

» **When planning your response, consider what it means to engage with, consume or read a media narrative. Engagement refers to how an audience emotionally and cognitively connects with a narrative. Consumption refers to how an audience physically views a narrative. Reading refers to an audience's interpretation and understanding of a narrative.**

Question 15

Sample response

Selected media narrative: *Breakfast at Tiffany's* (1961)

The depiction of Mr Yunioshi in Blake Edwards' classic film adaptation of *Breakfast at Tiffany's* may provoke disparate readings depending on when the film is viewed. Critics have suggested that the original audiences of 1961 may have seen the character played by white comedy actor Mickey Rooney, who dressed in yellow face for the role, through the lens of the 'Yellow Peril'; that is, the fear that East Asian people may pose a threat to Western culture. Therefore, audiences of this context may have been entertained to see Holly Golightly emasculate him as she responds to his angry, accented yelling by demurely stating, 'Don't be angry, you dear little man'. In contrast, in 2019 critic Romona Comet said of watching the performance, 'I felt taken completely out of the experience, finding myself watching a painfully unfunny performance of a racial stereotype'. Likewise, Asian American activist Ursula Liang labelled the film 'a minstrel show of racist ideology'. Furthermore, in 2022, acknowledgement of escalating anti-Asian sentiment in the United Kingdom led Channel 5 to remove scenes featuring the character from the film before it aired on their streaming service.

Mark allocation: 6 marks

- 6 marks: The student has provided a sophisticated discussion of how a media narrative may been read by two different audiences. They have used a specific, detailed example from the narrative, alongside contextual information for each of the audiences, to support the possible audience readings. The response clearly contrasts the two possible readings and outlines how and why these readings may have occurred. Effective application of media language is evident in the response.
- 5 marks: The student has provided a detailed discussion of how a media narrative may have been read by two different audiences. They have used a specific example from the narrative, alongside contextual information for each of the audiences, to support the possible audience readings. The response contrasts the two possible readings and outlines how and why these readings may have occurred. Thorough use of appropriate media language is evident in the response.
- 4 marks: The student has provided a clear discussion of how a media narrative may have been read by two different audiences. They have used an example from the narrative, alongside contextual information for each of the audiences, to support the possible audience readings. The response considers two possible readings and outlines how and why these readings may have occurred. Appropriate application of media language is evident in the response.
- 3 marks: The student has provided a general discussion of how a media narrative may have been read by two different audiences. They have used a basic example from the narrative and broadly outlined some contextual information for the audiences. The response considers two possible readings. Some application of media language is evident in the response.
- 2 marks: The student has provided a limited discussion of how a media narrative may have been read by two different audiences. They may have used a limited example from the narrative and outlined one context or given a brief overview of two contexts with little or no description. An attempt to use media language is evident; however, this may be with some inaccuracies.
- 1 mark: The student has provided an incomplete or very limited response that answers some part of the question. Little or no use of media language is evident in the response.

Question 16

Sample response

Selected media narrative: *The Swimmers* (2022)

In Sally El Hosaini's *The Swimmers*, sound is used to highlight the strength shown by protagonist Yusra as she flees her home country of Syria amid the refugee crisis of 2015. The song 'Titanium' by David Guetta featuring Sia is used as a motif, with El Hosaini using key lyrics to explore Yusra's character development. When Yusra is floating in the water, attempting to pull her overloaded boat to safety, a slow-motion shot of Yusra swimming through pelting rain is paired with dialogue from her father, who tells her to 'find your lane, swim your race'. This cuts to a shot of Yusra floating on her back, singing quietly along to the 'Titanium' lyrics, 'I'm bulletproof / nothing to lose', which is intercut with a fleeting flashback of a joyful family gathering. Two more similar sequences follow before the final sound clip plays, with Sia singing a confident 'You shoot me down / but I won't fall / I am Titanium'. As these lyrics are heard, El Hosaini shows Yusra wake from her stupor to see that land has become visible. This scene communicates that Yusra's limits are being tested but that she has the inner strength and determination required to get her family to safety. The song lyrics reflect the figurative and literal battles she faces in her life as a Syrian refugee and suggest that the messages her father instilled in her as her swimming coach have become useful in an entirely different context.

Note: This sample response is of a higher level than a typical student response to show the range of detail that can be used to answer this question.

Mark allocation: 6 marks

- 6 marks: The student has provided a sophisticated analysis of how one media code and one media convention work together to convey meaning in a media narrative. A specific, detailed example from the narrative has been provided that clearly demonstrates the code and convention working in conjunction. The student has analysed the meaning that may have been conveyed to an audience in this example, offering sophisticated insight into the filmmaker's possible intentions and demonstrating confident knowledge of the media narrative. Effective application of media language is evident in the response.
- 5 marks: The student has provided a detailed analysis of how one media code and one media convention work together to convey meaning in a media narrative. A detailed example from the narrative has been provided that demonstrates the code and convention working in conjunction. The student has analysed the meaning that may have been conveyed to an audience in this example, offering insight into the filmmaker's possible intentions and demonstrating strong knowledge of the media narrative. Thorough use of appropriate media language is evident in the response.
- 4 marks: The student has provided a clear analysis of how one media code and one media convention work together to convey meaning in a media narrative. An example from the narrative has been provided that demonstrates the code and convention working in conjunction. The student has outlined the meaning that may have been conveyed to an audience in this example, considering the filmmaker's possible intentions and demonstrating knowledge of the media narrative. Appropriate application of media language is evident in the response.

- 3 marks: The student has provided a general discussion of how one media code and one media convention work together to convey meaning in a media narrative, with an example. The student has outlined the meaning that may have been conveyed to an audience in this example, demonstrating some consideration of the filmmaker's possible intentions and appropriate knowledge of the media narrative. Some application of media language is evident in the response.
- 2 marks: The student has provided a limited discussion of how one media code and one media convention work together to convey meaning in a media narrative, with an example. The student has broadly suggested how the example demonstrates the code and convention, with reference to how meaning may have been conveyed. An attempt to use media language is evident; however, this may be with some inaccuracies.
- 1 mark: The student has provided an incomplete or very limited response that answers some part of the question. Little or no use of media language is evident in the response.

TIP

» **The examiner should know from the beginning of your response which media code and convention you will be discussing. Ensure these are clearly identified in the first sentence or two of your response.**

Unit 3 | Area of Study 1 Narratives and their contexts Section B

Question 1

Sample response

In *Moonlight*, Jenkins uses a range of codes and conventions to construct his protagonist, Chiron, as a representation of a young Black man coming to terms with his sexuality.

Moonlight is presented as a triptych, with Chiron's coming-of-age story separated into three distinct stages – 'Little', 'Chiron' and 'Black' – that assist in conveying the idea that Chiron is able to grow from a shy, unsure child (portrayed by Alex Hibbert) to a tortured, lost teen (Ashton Sanders) and lastly, into a conflicted but hopeful man (Trevante Rhodes). In order to more effectively portray Chiron's arc and changes in his journey, Jenkins made the unconventional decision to prevent the three actors from meeting one another or spending time together during filming. This ensured that Chiron's growth was reflected in the actors' acting styles, including their gait, posture and facial expressions. Hibbert's interpretation of Chiron, for example, sees him move with a hunched, stumbling gait as he escapes a soccer game with local boys, highlighting his uncertainty and discomfort with males his own age. Jenkins also uses mise en scène with his choice of colour and costuming. When Chiron is younger, he wears predominantly white clothing that is loose and ill-fitting, emphasising his innocence and vulnerability. The scenes in his home with his mother feature harsh, expressionistic lighting with yellowish tones, highlighting Chrion's feelings of oppression, and the tense, unstable environment due to his mother's neglect and addiction. In the 'Chiron' chapter, Sanders portrays Chiron's inner pain as he lopes down the middle of the road, his head lowered, on his way home from school. Framed from behind in a tracking shot, this image conveys the way Chiron has closed himself off from the world. His costume, such as his school uniform, is still oversized, indicating that it acts almost as a form of physical protection against the relentless bullying he receives at school due to his non-conforming behaviour. By Chiron's final transformation, Rhodes' imposing, muscular figure conveys the dramatic physical change his character has undergone. Chiron also wears tighter, more form fitting clothing to emphasise his muscular physique as well as tattoos, gold chains and grills, signalling his departure from the shy, introverted teen he was. However, as he moves from his car to the diner to meet Kevin (André Holland), Rhodes still walks with a slightly self-conscious stride, rubbing his head with one hand and shoving his hands into his pockets. In the film's final scene, Chiron is seen resting his head on Kevin's shoulder; Rhodes' gaze is fixed on the ground as Holland gently strokes his scalp. The contrast between this shot, and the first moment we see Chiron, running in a desperate scramble to get away from neighbourhood bullies, exemplifies the significant growth Chiron has experienced as he finds the freedom to express his sexual identity openly.

Mark allocation: 15 marks

- 14–15 marks: The student has provided a detailed and sophisticated response that develops an insightful analysis of how codes and conventions are used in the construction and/or representation of ideas in a media narrative. The student has used specific, detailed examples to support their ideas, and has employed highly appropriate media language throughout their response.
- 12–13 marks: The student has provided a detailed and thorough response that develops a well-considered analysis of how codes and conventions are used in the construction and/or representation of ideas in a media narrative. The student has used specific examples to support their analysis, and has employed appropriate media language throughout their response.
- 9–11 marks: The student has provided a clear and relevant response that develops a sound analysis of how codes and conventions are used in the construction and/or representation of ideas in a media narrative. The student has used appropriate examples to support their ideas, and has employed media language throughout their response.
- 7–8 marks: The student has provided a competent response that develops a general analysis of how codes and conventions are used in the construction and/or representation of ideas in a media narrative. The student has used examples to support their ideas, and has employed some media language throughout their response.
- 5–6 marks: The student has provided a general response that develops some analysis of how codes and conventions are used in the construction and/or representation of ideas in a media narrative. The student may have used broad examples to support their ideas, and has employed limited media language throughout their response.
- 3–4 marks: The student has provided a basic response that shows some analysis of how codes and conventions are used in the construction and/or representation of ideas in a media narrative. The student may have used simplistic examples to support their ideas. Minimal use of media language is evident, impacting the clarity of the response.
- 1–2 marks: The student has provided a limited response that demonstrates some knowledge of the role codes and conventions play in conveying meaning to an audience.

TIPS

» **Select key scenes that allow you to delve deep into the analysis of codes and conventions, and be very specific in your analysis to support your discussion. Remember, the reader may not be familiar with the narrative, so you need to be explicit in your examples.**

» **Ensure you explain exactly what meaning or ideas have been constructed, rather than simply identifying ideas.**

» **Use specific terminology to clearly illustrate your discussion.**

Question 2

Sample response

The relationship between media narratives and their audiences can be seen in elements of the production, distribution, consumption and reception of the film *Crazy Rich Asians* (Jon M. Chu, 2018).

When the film adaptation of Kevin Kwan's novel *Crazy Rich Asians* was announced, it became a highly anticipated cinematic release, due in part to it being the first Hollywood film with an all-Asian cast since *The Joy Luck Club* in 1993. However, the distribution of the film was as widely discussed as its racial representation. In an article for *The Hollywood Reporter*, journalists Rebecca Sun and Rebecca Ford reported that Kwan and Jon M. Chu turned down a distribution offer by Netflix that meant Kwan 'could have moved to an island and never worked another day', in favour of a significantly smaller offer by Warner Bros in order to ensure their film obtained a cinematic release. This demonstrates the film creators' understanding of the relationship between the media and its audience: they espoused the importance of Asian Americans seeing themselves represented on the big screen. This is reflected in some of the key scenes of the film, such as when Rachel (Constance Wu) and Eleanor (Michelle Yeoh) play a heated game of mahjong. The intricate gameplay, use of traditional Chinese tiles and strategic maneuvering are authentic elements of the game that resonate with Asian audiences familiar with its cultural significance. The symbolism of each move and the tension between the characters reflect the complexities of family dynamics and cultural expectations in Asian societies. Rachel also wears a red dress in scenes in the film, a colour typically associated with luck in Chinese culture. When she is seen wearing the dress by members of Nick's family, one of the characters jokes about red being lucky 'only if you're an envelope', a culturally specific reference to the practice of giving red envelopes as gifts for Chinese New Year or milestone events such as weddings or births. Chu sought to engage Asian Americans by dropping in Easter eggs that may have enhanced Asian audience members' experience of the narrative. For example, in the scene where Nick (Henry Golding) and Rachel are spotted in a cafe by one of Nick's family friends, the ensuing flurry of direct messages that pops up on the screen contains multiple cultural references. The message bubbles contain messages such as 'Looks ABC' and 'Wah, so many Rachel Chus, lah', using slang from Chinese American communities and Singlish phrasing to add authenticity to the film and personalise it for Asian audiences. This impacts the reception of the film for the modern Asian audience, helping to build a personal connection between the audience and the characters and scenes, as demonstrated by journalist Stephanie Foo's comment, 'I heard people talking like [the characters] had in my house growing up, and ... waterworks'.

Mark allocation: 15 marks

- 14–15 marks: The student has provided a detailed and sophisticated response that develops an insightful analysis of the relationship between media narratives and their audiences, referring insightfully to at least one of the following: the production, distribution, consumption or reception of a media narrative. The student has used specific, detailed examples to support their ideas and has employed highly appropriate media language throughout their response.

- 12–13 marks: The student has provided a detailed and thorough response that develops a well-considered analysis of the relationship between media narratives and their audiences, referring strongly to at least one of the following: the production, distribution, consumption or reception of a media narrative. The student has used specific examples to support their ideas, and has employed appropriate media language throughout their response.
- 9–11 marks: The student has provided a clear and relevant response that develops a sound analysis of the relationship between media narratives and their audiences, referring coherently to at least one of the following: the production, distribution, consumption or reception of a media narrative. The student has used appropriate examples to support their ideas and has employed media language throughout their response.
- 7–8 marks: The student has provided a competent response that develops a general analysis of the relationship between media narratives and their audiences, making relevant references to at least one of the following: the production, distribution, consumption or reception of a media narrative. The student has used examples to support their ideas and has employed some media language throughout their response.
- 5–6 marks: The student has provided a general response that develops some analysis of the relationship between media narratives and their audiences, making basic references to at least one of the following: the production, distribution, consumption or reception of a media narrative. The student has used broad examples to support their ideas and has employed limited media language throughout their response.
- 3–4 marks: The student has provided a basic response that shows some analysis of the relationship between media narratives and their audiences, making basic references to at least one of the following: the production, distribution, consumption or reception of a media narrative. The student may have used simplistic examples to support their ideas. Minimal use of media language is evident, impacting the clarity of the response.
- 1–2 marks: The student has provided a limited or incomplete response that demonstrates some knowledge of the relationship between media narratives and their audiences, making little or no reference to at least one of the following: the production, distribution, consumption or reception of a media narrative.

Question 3

Sample response

An audience's engagement with and reading of a media narrative can be significantly impacted by contextual factors, such as the discourses that are occurring in society at a given time. The bonus episode of *Euphoria* (Levinson, 2019), 'Trouble Don't Last Always', released in 2020, explicitly aims to reflect discourses relating to racial injustice. Furthermore, the episode was designed around COVID-19 restrictions and, as a result, reflects a world that had become very familiar to audiences at the time. An audience consuming the narrative at its time of release may have therefore experienced heightened engagement with the narrative and have agreed with a dominant reading of it due to how clearly it is shaped by its context.

The episode, which follows 2019's Season 1, was created after production of Season 2 was stalled due to the pandemic, an element of its institutional context.

While the series is known for its chaotic energy and frenetic crowd shots of teenagers partying, the special episode almost entirely takes place in a singular setting with just two characters: Rue (Zendaya Coleman), the show's protagonist, and Ali (Colman Domingo), her Narcotics Anonymous sponsor. In the absence of the series' usual features, creator Sam Levinson uses the episode to facilitate a more detailed and intimate discussion of the addiction that grips Rue, which was a catalyst for significant conflict and action in Season 1. Audiences at the time of release may have engaged more readily with this pared back version of the show due to their immediate understanding of the reasons behind its construction.

The episode is also shaped by the political context in which it was made. In May 2020, racial tensions in America came to a head with the death of George Floyd at the hands of the police in Minneapolis, after an officer knelt on his neck and back for nearly ten minutes, depriving him of oxygen. The incident made headlines worldwide, sparking a wave of Black Lives Matter protests that demanded justice for Black Americans. Coleman was vocal in her own support for the cause, promoting the Week of Action in Defense of Black Lives schedule on her Instagram feed with the caption 'Do not stop applying pressure …', along with other clips and resources promoting the fight for Black people's freedom. These tensions were reflected in the dialogue between Ali and Rue in the episode, as Ali laments the way 'revolutions are fought and won so damn fast that the people don't even have time to implement change' and expresses his frustration at the corporate response – 'Chinese Muslims are sewing these Kaepernick sneakers for seven cents an hour, and [Nike is] tellin' me my Black ass matters'. The timeliness of this messaging may have ensured audiences were more easily able to adopt a dominant reading of the narrative. In this way, Levinson's work – with its purpose of addressing social injustices and building on the lives of the *Euphoria* characters, despite a halted production schedule – is clearly impacted by social, institutional and political contexts.

Mark allocation: 15 marks

- 14–15 marks: The student has provided a detailed and sophisticated response that develops an insightful discussion of how the context in which a media narrative is consumed can impact audience engagement or reading. The response refers insightfully to the relationship between a media narrative and audiences with considered reference to the narrative's contexts. The student has used specific, detailed examples to support their ideas and employed highly appropriate media language throughout their response. The media narrative used as the basis of the discussion has been addressed to an excellent standard.
- 12–13 marks: The student has provided a detailed and thorough response that develops a well-considered discussion of how the context in which a media narrative is consumed can impact audience engagement or reading. The response refers strongly to the relationship between a media narrative and audiences with considered reference to the narrative's contexts. The student has used specific examples to support their ideas and employed appropriate media language throughout their response. The media narrative used as the basis of the discussion has been addressed to a very high standard.

- 9–11 marks: The student has provided a clear and relevant response that develops a sound discussion of how the context in which a media narrative is consumed can impact audience engagement or reading. The response refers coherently to the relationship between a media narrative and audiences with appropriate reference to the narrative's contexts. The student has used appropriate examples to support their ideas and employed relevant media language throughout their response. The media narrative used as the basis of the discussion has been addressed to a very good standard.
- 7–8 marks: The student has provided a competent response that develops a general discussion of how the context in which a media narrative is consumed can impact audience engagement or reading. The response makes relevant reference to the relationship between a media narrative and audiences with reference to the narrative's contexts. The student has used examples to support their ideas and has employed some media language throughout their response. The media narrative used as the basis of the discussion has been addressed to a good standard.
- 5–6 marks: The student has provided a general response that develops some discussion of how the context in which a media narrative is consumed can impact audience engagement or reading. The response references the relationship between a media narrative and audiences with some acknowledgment of the contexts. The student may have used broad examples to support their ideas and employed limited media language throughout their response. The media narrative used as the basis of the discussion has been addressed generally.
- 3–4 marks: The student has provided a basic response that shows some discussion of how the context in which a media narrative is consumed can impact audience engagement or reading. The student may have used simplistic examples to support their response. Minimal use of media language is evident, impacting the clarity of the response.
- 1–2 marks: The student has provided a limited or incomplete response that demonstrates some knowledge of how the context in which a media narrative is consumed can impact audience engagement. Limited or no media language has been employed in the response.

TIP

» **When referring to narrative context in higher mark questions, provide some information about the context you are referring to. In this example, the context of Black Lives Matter is not only mentioned, it is explained, including how the racial tensions in 2020 arose after George Floyd's death.**

Question 4

Sample response

In Emerald Fennell's film *Promising Young Woman* (2020), sound and mise en scène are used in conjunction with setting, foreshadowing and symbolism to convey the idea that the male-centric discourse around rape culture is toxic and damaging to women.

The film's criticism of the normalisation and excusing of sexual violence is exemplified in the film's third act as Cassie (Carey Mulligan) arrives at the bachelor party for Al (Chris Lowell). As she gets out of her car and begins to walk towards the isolated cabin, Anthony Willis' score is an ominous string arrangement of Britney Spears' song 'Toxic'. The once upbeat, poppy smash hit has been reimagined into a creepy, slowed down orchestral arrangement to create a 'very unpleasant setting', according to Willis. This, alongside the lyrical association foreshadows to the audience that the toxic behaviour Cassie is about to encounter at the hands of male characters who have, at earlier points in the narrative, been described as 'really nice' guys, may become sinister and dangerous, especially when they are physically removed from other members of society who may act as witnesses. Cassie is wearing a white nurse's uniform with white stockings, and walks barefoot at a funereal pace holding red high heels in one hand. The juxtaposition between the natural setting of the surrounding forest and her artificial appearance is jarring, reflecting the way patriarchal systems and the male gaze encourage women to alter their appearance to attract men. Unlike previous scenes, which Fennel balances with perfect symmetry, this scene places Cassie on the left of the frame, creating a sense of imbalance and unease for the audience. The longshot used at this moment appears to swallow Cassie, making her small and insignificant within the frame to foreshadow her worth in the eyes of the men at the bachelor party, which ultimately leads to her mistreatment, death and brutal disposal.

This level of meaning and symbolism relies on the audience's contextual awareness. *Promising Young Woman* was produced and set in the wake of the #MeToo movement, which resurged in 2017 after the infamous Harvey Weinstein scandals, where he was convicted of sexually assaulting more than 80 women. Alongside an emphasis on speaking out against abusers, the movement also prompted discussions surrounding victim blaming, consent and accountability. The text reflects messages that are explored in fourth-wave feminism as women call for systemic change and recognition of rape culture in Western society. Released in late 2020, Fennell's film relies upon the global feminist discourse and social and political contexts to imbue her text with further meaning.

Mark allocation: 15 marks

- 14–15 marks: The student has provided a detailed and sophisticated response that develops an insightful analysis of how media codes and conventions in a media narrative are used to convey meaning to an audience. The student has used specific, detailed examples to support their ideas, and has thoroughly linked their response to at least two contexts, which may include social, cultural, institutional, historical, economic or political contexts. They have employed highly appropriate media language throughout their response.

- 12–13 marks: The student has provided a detailed and thorough response that develops a well-considered discussion of how media codes and conventions in a media narrative are used to convey meaning to an audience. The student has used specific examples to support their ideas, and has made strong links in their response to at least two contexts, which may include social, cultural, institutional, historical, economic or political contexts. They have employed appropriate media language throughout their response.
- 9–11 marks: The student has provided a clear and relevant response that develops a sound analysis of how media codes and conventions in a media narrative are used to convey meaning to an audience. The student has used appropriate examples to support their ideas and has competently linked their response to at least two contexts, which may include social, cultural, institutional, historical, economic or political contexts. They have employed relevant media language throughout their response.
- 7–8 marks: The student has provided a competent response that develops a general analysis of how media codes and conventions in a media narrative are used to convey meaning to an audience. However, the response may be lacking in specific detail. The student has used examples to support their ideas and has soundly linked their response to social, cultural, institutional, historical, economic or political contexts. They have employed some media language throughout their response.
- 5–6 marks: The student has provided a general response that develops some analysis of how media codes and conventions in a media narrative are used to convey meaning to an audience. The student may have used broad examples to support their ideas and may vaguely link their response to social, cultural, institutional, historical, economic or political contexts. They have employed limited media language throughout their response.
- 3–4 marks: The student has provided a basic response that develops some analysis of how media codes and conventions in a media narrative are used to convey meaning to an audience. The student may have used simplistic examples to support their ideas and made basic reference to social, cultural, institutional, historical, economic or political contexts. Minimal use of media language is evident, impacting the clarity of the response.
- 1–2 marks: The student has provided a limited or incomplete response that demonstrates some knowledge of the role media codes and conventions in media narratives play in conveying meaning to an audience. The response contains little or no reference to social, cultural, institutional, historical, economic or political contexts. The response contains limited or no examples or media language.

Unit 3 | Area of Study 2 Research, development and experimentation

Question 1

Sample response

In my own media production, *Chase*, I was inspired by the works of Christopher Nolan, particularly his use of non-linear storytelling to enhance narrative complexity and overall audience engagement. After watching films like *Memento* and *Inception*, I used the concept of in media res, structuring my film non-chronologically to help capture the confusion and disorientation of my main protagonist who is trying to figure out where his brother has disappeared to. To do this, one technique I utilised was the juxtaposition of past and present timelines, even using colour grading to differentiate between flashbacks and the present, much like in *Memento*. By incorporating Nolan's distinctive use of non-linear storytelling, I was able to provide my audience with my main character's backstory and establish his relationship with his missing brother. I used transitions between the past and the present to make viewers suspicious that he may have had something to do with his own disappearance. By altering the time structure, I built suspense and momentum for the audience, honouring Nolan's style of keeping viewers engaged until the final moment.

Mark allocation: 4 marks

- 4 marks: The student has provided a clear and detailed discussion of the way they have used a technique or idea of another creator in their own production. The student made clear links to the creator and used specific and relevant examples demonstrating a deep understanding of both the chosen creator's style/idea and their own production goals. Thorough use of appropriate media language is evident in the response.
- 3 marks: The student has provided a clear discussion of the way they have used a technique or idea of another creator in their own production. They have provided relevant examples and made links to the creator. The student has demonstrated a reasonable understanding of both the chosen creator's style/idea and their own production goals. Some application of media language is evident in the response.
- 2 marks: The student has provided a general discussion of the way they used a technique or idea of another creator in their own production. Some examples have been used but they lack specificity. An attempt to use media language is evident; however, this may be with some inaccuracies.
- 1 mark: The student has provided a limited discussion of the way they used a technique or idea of another creator in their own production. The student has referred generally to their production and given a broad or unrelated example of how the technique or idea was used. An attempt to use media language is evident; however, this is mostly irrelevant or incorrect.

Question 2a.

Sample response

Selected media form: The media form I explored in my pre-production was audio (podcasting).

Mark allocation: 1 mark

- 1 mark: The student has clearly identified the media form they explored in pre-production.

Question 2b.

Sample response

My research and investigation of the podcasting medium and existing media products such as *Serial* and *Criminal* played a crucial role in shaping the planning of my production and the narrative I wanted to tell. I wanted my podcast to be a mock true crime podcast where two students investigate a crime in their local neighbourhood. During my research, I looked at the various storytelling techniques and formats of the podcasts that I enjoyed listening to in order to ascertain the strategies they used to engage audiences, such as plot twists and point of view. This inspired me to tell the story from the perspective of two self-proclaimed 'true crime addicts'– best friends who believe their knowledge of true crime podcasts can help them solve the crime. Telling the story from the perspective of the amateur teenage detectives added another layer of engagement as my primarily teenage audience discovers the clues at the same time as them.

In my observations, I also noted how in the absence of visual elements, I would need to incorporate a range of diegetic and non-diegetic sounds. When I had my two hosts change locations from the library to the canteen, I included the diegetic sounds of students playing, laughing and talking at lunchtime and then added in sound effects such as the bell ringing to signal a shift in the discussion. In doing this, I aimed to immerse my listeners in the world of the podcast which is primarily set in a high school. When listening to *Serial*, *S Town* and *Missing and Murdered*, I observed how the hosts had interviews with the accused (such as Adnan Syed) as well as those close to the victims, in the interest of showing both sides of the story. To imitate this, I incorporated personal narratives and interviews with the staff members and students who claimed to be impacted by the crime in some way. I did this to humanise victims, suspects and witnesses in order to create a deeper emotional connection with my audience.

Note: This sample response is of a higher level than a typical student response, in order to show the range of detail that can be used to answer the question.

Mark allocation: 4 marks

- 4 marks: The student has provided a clear and detailed discussion of the way they have used research or investigation of their chosen media form and existing media products to shape the planning of their production and the narrative they wanted to tell. The student made clear links to the form and products and used specific and relevant examples demonstrating a deep understanding of the chosen media form and their own production goals. Thorough use of appropriate media language is evident in the response.

- 3 marks: The student has provided a clear discussion of how the research or investigation of their chosen media form and existing media products shaped the planning of their production and the narrative they wanted to tell. They have provided relevant examples and made links to the chosen media form and products and their own production goals. Some application of media language is evident in the response.
- 2 marks: The student has provided a general discussion of the way the research or investigation of their chosen media form and existing media products shaped the planning of their production and the narrative they wanted to tell. Some examples have been used but lack specificity. An attempt to use media language is evident; however, this may be with some inaccuracies.
- 1 mark: The student has provided a limited discussion of the way the research or investigation of their chosen media form and existing media products shaped the planning of their production and the narrative they wanted to tell. The student has referred generally to their production and given a broad or unrelated example of how the technique or idea was used. An attempt to use media language is evident; however, this is mostly irrelevant or incorrect.

TIP

» **Be specific when referring to your investigation or research by identifying exactly what you researched.**

Question 3

Sample response

> One step I took to develop my idea for my media product was research and analysis of my chosen media form and other media products.
>
> Another step I took to develop my idea was brainstorming different concepts that aligned with my own personal interests, skills and goals.

Mark allocation: 2 marks

- 2 marks: The student has clearly identified two steps they took to develop an idea for their media production.
- 1 mark: The student has either clearly identified one step they took to develop an idea or they have referenced two steps but only vaguely.

Question 4

Sample response

For my first production experiment, I chose to explore split-screen editing as a technique to show the juxtaposition of my character's motives and the repercussions of his decisions. Experimenting with split-screen editing has sharpened my understanding of visual composition and framing techniques, and allowed me to create a parallel storyline in a scene in my production. By using Adobe Premier Pro, I created mock scenes and sequences to test various split-screen layouts and effects, allowing me to refine my skills and develop a deeper understanding of how to effectively use the program to help me with my final project. I initially struggled with how to seamlessly blend multiple footage sources but, after watching YouTube tutorials, I was able to synchronise both the visual and audio sequences and create smooth transitions, a skill that I ultimately used in my production.

Mark allocation: 4 marks

- 4 marks: The student has provided a clear and detailed discussion of the way one production experiment helped refine or develop their skills in their selected media form. The student has used specific and relevant examples. Thorough use of appropriate media language is evident in the response.
- 3 marks: The student has provided a clear discussion of the way one production experiment helped refine or develop their skills in their selected media form. The answer is supported with relevant examples. Some application of media language is evident in the response.
- 2 marks: The student has provided a general discussion of the way one production experiment helped refine or develop their skills in their selected media form. Some examples have been used but lack specificity. An attempt to use media language is evident; however, this may be with some inaccuracies.
- 1 mark: The student has provided a limited discussion of the way one production experiment helped refine or develop their skills in their selected media form. Broad or unrelated examples are provided. An attempt to use media language is evident; however, this is mostly irrelevant or incorrect.

TIP

» **The question only asks you to discuss one of your two production experiments. If you discuss both, only discussion of one experiment will be taken into consideration during marking.**

Question 5

Sample response

> In my research stage, I looked at the genre and style of various documentaries, which helped to inform my final media product, *Voices for Change*, which aimed to explore the views, experiences and activism of young people fighting for climate change awareness. Through research, I identified several subgenres within the documentary genre, including observational documentaries, expository documentaries and participatory documentaries such as *RiP: A Remix Manifesto*. In my own documentary, I wanted to engage the voices of my local community, so this research informed me on how to create a media product that reflected the views of the people that my story was about. I also researched and watched *Our Planet*, one of the first documentaries to use storytelling strategies to be an explicit 'call to action'. This influenced my own production, as one of my main objectives was to inform my audience of the consequences for us and our environment if we don't implement change. I wanted to make 'green mainstream' and present some solutions to the global crisis. Documentary research also informed my understanding of visual aesthetics and cinematography techniques used in the genre. By observing the vérité style of observational documentaries like *Hoop Dreams* to provoke and reveal truth, I used similar improvisational concepts in *Voices for Change* by allowing things to unfold naturally on camera, such as an interview with a local politician.

Mark allocation: 4 marks

- 4 marks: The student has provided a clear and detailed discussion of the way research into their media form's genre/style helped to develop their own production. The student has used specific and relevant examples. Thorough use of appropriate media language is evident in the response.
- 3 marks: The student has provided a clear discussion of the way research into their media form's genre/style helped to develop their own production. The answer is supported with relevant examples. Some application of media language is evident in the response.
- 2 marks: The student has provided a general discussion of the way research into their media form's genre/style helped to develop their own production. Some examples have been used but lack specificity. An attempt to use media language is evident; however, this may be with some inaccuracies.
- 1 mark: The student has provided a limited discussion of the way research into their media form's genre/style helped to develop their own production. Broad or unrelated examples are provided. An attempt to use media language is evident; however, this is mostly irrelevant or incorrect.

Question 6

Sample response

I studied the media practitioner Sam Mendes and his use of the code mise en scène, particularly in the film *American Beauty*. Mendes uses mise en scène to reveal aspects of his characters' personalities, to foreshadow events and also to demonstrate power dynamics. In the meeting scene of *American Beauty*, Mendes shoots Lester (Kevin Spacey) in a wide shot where Lester only takes up a small part of the frame. He is shot from a low angle which is designed to look like a point-of-view shot from his boss, Brad, who in contrast is filmed in close-ups where he is centred in the frame and takes up the majority of the space in the shots. In the background of Lester's shots, the decor is grey and dull with a dying plant in the corner and dim, low-key lighting suggesting that Lester is both powerless and miserable at his job. To add to this, the vertical blinds cast shadows that create a jail or cage-like appearance, emphasising Lester's pessimistic view of his workplace.

This influenced a scene in my music video where I employed similar ideas with my main protagonist in the principal's office. My main character Kate does not want to be at school and instead wants to pursue her dream of being a pop star. When shooting a scene in the principal's office, I also shot the character from high angles and used wide shots to make her appear helpless and alone. When the principal stands over Kate, I mimicked the scene in *American Beauty* and shot the principal from an extreme low angle to make her appear intimidating and scary to Kate. I used a gavel as a prop on the principal's desk to indicate to the audience that Kate feels judged and the school is a prison for her. The furniture, Kate's uniform and the principal's clothing are black and white, while Kate wears a bright pink headband and red lipstick to show that she does not fit in with the simplistic and archaic school setting.

Note: This sample response is of a higher level than a typical student response, in order to show the range of detail that can be used to answer the question.

Mark allocation: 5 marks

- 4–5 marks: The student has provided a detailed and insightful discussion of how a media creator they researched used a code or convention to create meaning and how this influenced their own production. The student has provided specific and relevant examples. Effective media language is used in the response.
- 3 marks: The student has provided a clear and relevant discussion of how a media creator they researched used a code or convention to create meaning and how this influenced their own production. The student has provided some relevant examples. Relevant media language has been used in the response.
- 2 marks: The student has provided a general discussion of how a media creator they researched used a code or convention to create meaning and how this influenced their own production. Some media language has been used in the response.
- 1 mark: The student has provided a weak example of how a media creator they researched used a code or convention to create meaning and how this influenced their own production. Limited or no media language has been used in the response.

Question 7

Sample response

During the research, development and experimentation stage, I developed the skill of invisible cuts. I researched and drew inspiration from the films *Birdman* and *1917* because in my proposed product, a short drama film, I wanted to follow a protagonist through a conflict without visible editing. The art of invisible cutting allows the audience to be fully immersed in the conflict on-screen, maintaining constant tension from the start of the sequence until its conclusion, which I believed to be an effective way of raising the stakes in a drama film that has a very limited run time.

Mark allocation: 3 marks

- 3 marks: The student has provided a clear and relevant explanation of how an identified skill relates to either their proposed media product or their selected media form. Relevant media language is evident in the response.
- 2 marks: The student has provided a general example of how an identified skill relates to either their proposed media product or their selected media form. Some media language is evident in the response.
- 1 mark: The student has provided a limited description of a skill developed. Little or no connection has been established with their proposed media product or their selected media form. Limited or no media language is evident in the response.

Question 8

Sample response

Experimentation with equipment, media technologies, and processes is an important part of the production process to develop or refine skills. By exploring new equipment or media technologies, media professionals are able to explore new ideas and techniques that ultimately lead to better storytelling. For me, by familiarising myself with the capabilities and limitations of different cameras and audio recording devices, I was able to choose equipment that I was comfortable with and research YouTube tutorials on using equipment or technologies that I lacked confidence in. Through the trial-and-error experimentation process, I was able to overcome technical challenges and find creative solutions for my production.

Mark allocation: 3 marks

- 3 marks: A thoughtful response that clearly explains why experimentation with equipment, media technologies, and processes is important in the production of a media product. Relevant media language is used in the response.
- 2 marks: A general response that explains why experimentation with equipment, media technologies, and processes is important in the production of a media product. Some media language is used in the response.
- 1 mark: A limited response that attempts to explain why experimentation with equipment, media technologies, and processes is important in the production of a media product, but may not provide any additional explanation. Limited or no media language has been used in the response.

Question 9a.

Sample response

> An example of media equipment would be a DSLR camera.

Mark allocation: 1 mark

- 1 mark: An example of media equipment has been correctly identified.

TIP

» **Equipment may include (but is not limited to) tripods, lighting, cameras, specialised lenses, light reflectors, dolly or a backdrop.**

Question 9b.

Sample response

> An example of a media technology would be Photoshop.

Mark allocation: 1 mark

- 1 mark: An example of a media technology has been correctly identified.

TIP

» **Technology may include (but is not limited to) Adobe Illustrator, Adobe Photoshop, Adobe InDesign, Adobe Lightroom, Adobe Premiere Pro, laptops, scanners or other software.**

Question 9c.

Sample response

> An example of a media process is the distribution of a media product to the intended audience, such as by uploading it to YouTube and other platforms.

Mark allocation: 1 mark

- 1 mark: An example of a media process has been correctly identified.

Question 10

Sample response

When researching zines, my chosen media form, I immersed myself in a variety of feminist zines which was the genre I wanted to primarily focus on. After reading and researching zines such as *Stigma Zine* and *Girls Get Busy*, I not only explored the diverse range of themes, voices and perspectives within feminist media culture but also identified a particular skill I wanted to develop for my zine: layout and design. These zines offer unique insights on the power of visual storytelling and feature innovative and dynamic layouts with colour, imagery, white space and typography, as well as hand-drawn artwork. By researching these zines in my pre-production stage, I was able to recognise the creative layouts and design techniques and wanted to develop my own layout skills to express my feminist beliefs and amplify marginalised voices. To hone and develop these skills, I decided to do one of my production experiments on visual hierarchy, balance and white space on Adobe InDesign, and I refined these skills even further for my final project.

Mark allocation: 4 marks

- 4 marks: The student has provided a clear and detailed discussion of the way research into their chosen media form and products helped to identify a skill they wanted to develop or refine for their own production. The student has used specific and relevant examples. Thorough use of appropriate media language is evident in the response.
- 3 marks: The student has provided a clear discussion of the way research into their chosen media form and products helped them to identify a skill they wanted to develop or refine for their own production. The answer is supported with relevant examples. Some application of media language is evident in the response.
- 2 marks: The student has provided a general discussion of the way research into their chosen media form and products helped to identify a skill they wanted to develop or refine for their own production. Some examples have been used but lack specificity. An attempt to use media language is evident; however, this may be with some inaccuracies.
- 1 mark: The student has provided a limited discussion of the way research into their chosen media form and products helped to identify a skill they wanted to refine or develop for their own production. Broad or unrelated examples are provided. An attempt to use media language is evident; however, this is mostly irrelevant or incorrect.

Question 11

Sample response

> For my production, *Amy Boulevard*, I decided to conduct my production experiments on lighting to help me capture the essence of a film noir style. To achieve this, I focused on lighting setups inspired by classic film noir aesthetics. To replicate film noir lighting on a budget, I explored cost-effective lighting solutions such as clamp lights, desk lamps and LED light panels from Bunnings. I practised positioning lights at extreme angles to cast deep shadows and sculpted three-dimensional forms, using household items like curtains or cardboard, to control spill and create pools of darkness. To enhance the mood in my scenes and emphasise the film noir genre, I experimented with practical effects like casting shadows through window blinds or using coloured gels to simulate the glow of neon lights, adding depth and atmosphere to my compositions.

Mark allocation: 3 marks

- 3 marks: A thoughtful response that clearly explains how the student's production experiments helped communicate their chosen genre/style to their intended audience. Relevant media language is used in the response.
- 2 marks: A general response that explains how the student's production experiments helped communicate their chosen genre/style to their intended audience. Some media language is used in the response.
- 1 mark: A limited response that attempts to explain how the student's production experiments helped communicate their chosen genre/style to their intended audience but may not provide any additional explanation Limited or no media language has been used in the response.

Question 12

Sample response

> I looked into the works of Taika Waititi to inform my understanding of how structural and aesthetic qualities can be used to engage audiences. I learned that Waititi has incorporated wide-angle landscape shots into many of his films for comedic purposes. For example, in *Boy*, a wide shot of Alamein tunnelling his way out of prison and fighting prison guards in a humorously exaggerated manner engages the audience as spectators to this fantastic and unlikely scenario, while keeping them at a physical distance from the action to highlight the unreliable nature of Boy's memory. Furthermore, Waititi consistently employs the structural qualities of a coming-of-age story in his films to build his narratives around a familiar and relatable framework. The opening sequences of each film introduce the characters and their flaws, such as Jojo's short-sighted fanaticism in *Jojo Rabbit*, in order to communicate to the audience the areas the protagonist must develop.

Mark allocation: 4 marks

- 4 marks: The student has provided two highly appropriate examples of structural and/or aesthetic qualities, referring to the genres, media practitioners, styles or products that they researched. They have linked these examples to the purpose of engaging audiences in a highly appropriate way. Effective media language is used in the response.
- 3 marks: The student has provided two clear examples of structural and/or aesthetic qualities, referring to the genres, media practitioners, styles or products that they researched. They have clearly linked these examples to the purpose of engaging audiences. Relevant media language is used in the response.
- 2 marks: The student has provided one detailed example, or two limited examples, of structural and/or aesthetic qualities, referring to the genres, media practitioners, styles or products that they researched. They have made some reference to audience engagement. Basic media language is used in the response.
- 1 mark: The student has identified a limited example of a structural or aesthetic quality, referring to the genres, media practitioners, styles or products that they researched. They may not have linked this to audience engagement. Limited or no media language is used in the response.

Note: If only one specific example is given, a maximum of two marks can be awarded.

Question 13

Sample response

> Selected media form: photography
>
> Throughout my research, I explored the various tools I could use to remove the backgrounds of images, to determine the most effective way to create graphics with transparent backgrounds. I tried Apple's 'remove background' feature, as well as Adobe Photoshop, Affinity Photo and an online background removal site. My research taught me how to batch edit background removal for simpler images, and how to remove complex backgrounds using the tools in each program. I also learned that my preference is to use Adobe Photoshop for this process.

Mark allocation: 3 marks

- 3 marks: The student has provided a thoughtful response that clearly explains how one component of their research relates to a skill required to produce a media form. The student has given relevant details that outline the information gathered from the research process and has summarised how their skills developed as a result. Relevant media language is used in the response.
- 2 marks: The student has provided a general response that explains how one component of their research relates to a skill required to produce a media form. The student has broadly outlined how their skills developed as a result of their research. Some media language is used in the response.
- 1 mark: The student has provided a limited response that attempts to explain how their research relates to a skill required to produce a media form but may not provide any additional explanation. Limited or no media language has been used in the response.

Question 14

Sample response

While recording my podcast series, *ImmiGreat*, I kept a running sheet of notes with timecodes and content, marking down mistakes or interesting comments made by the speakers to be kept in or edited out of the final products. Because the series had a question-and-answer format with conversation between three speakers, there was a lot of content to sift through. By highlighting the best and least effective moments during recording, I was able to minimise the time I spent listening back and editing. For example, one of my speakers incorrectly used the idiom 'for all intents and purposes', instead saying 'for all intensive purposes'. I didn't want this to distract my audience, so I got the speaker to ask the question correctly, and later edited in this version. Ultimately, this helped me realise my production by ensuring the audio content I obtained from my speakers was relevant, entertaining and high quality.

Mark allocation: 5 marks

- 5 marks: The student has provided a detailed and insightful discussion of how a process that has been used to document the development of a media product has helped them create their media product. The student has given a specific and detailed example to support their discussion of how this process enabled them to realise their media production. Thorough use of appropriate media language is evident in the response.
- 4 marks: The student has provided a clear discussion of how a process that has been used to document the development of a media product has helped them create their media product. The student has given a detailed example to support their discussion of how this process enabled them to realise their media production. Appropriate application of media language is evident in the response.
- 3 marks: The student has provided a general discussion of how a process that has been used to document the development of a media product has helped them create their media product. The student has given an example to support their discussion of how this process enabled them to realise their media production. Some application of media language is evident in the response.
- 2 marks: The student has provided a limited discussion of how a process that has been used to document the development of a media product has helped them create their media product. The student has given a broad or unrelated example to support their discussion. An attempt to use media language is evident; however, this may be with some inaccuracies.
- 1 mark: The student has provided an incomplete or very limited response that answers some part of the question. Little or no use of media language is evident in the response.

Question 15

Sample response

> During the research, development and experimentation stage, I experimented with interviewing techniques to learn how to get the most effective responses from subjects as part of my preparation for documentary filmmaking. I used research to inform my practice and devised a series of questions to ask my peers about their preparations for the Year 12 formal. One technique that I used was to ask questions and pose prompts that required subjects to answer in full sentences and with insight instead of giving simple 'yes' or 'no' responses; for example, 'What do you think will be the best part of the night?' and 'Tell me about your date'. Creating interesting sound bites is an important part of documentary filmmaking because the absence of a script means there is an unpredictable variable that could result in a less engaging product. I saw this process as being crucial to eliminating that potential obstacle.

Mark allocation: 5 marks

- 5 marks: The student has provided a detailed and insightful example of how they developed one skill during their research, development and experimentation stage. They have linked this to their selected media form in a considered way. Highly relevant media language is used in the response.
- 4 marks: The student has provided a clear and relevant example of how they developed one skill during their research, development and experimentation stage. They have linked this to their selected media form in an appropriate way. Effective media language is used in the response.
- 3 marks: The student has provided an appropriate example of how they developed one skill during their research, development and experimentation stage. They have clearly linked this to their selected media form. Relevant media language is used in the response.
- 2 marks: The student has provided a general example of how they developed one skill during their research, development and experimentation stage. They have linked this to their selected media form in some way. Some media language is used in the response.
- 1 mark: The student has identified a limited example of one skill developed during their research, development and experimentation stage. They have not linked this to their selected media form. Limited or no media language is used in the response.

Unit 3 | Area of Study 3 Pre-production planning

Question 1

Sample response

When planning my production timeline, there were numerous factors I had to take into consideration. The first of these was my casting decision to work with a group of five fellow VCE students from my school. I have learnt the importance of maintaining flexibility in filming schedules when working with peers, given their tendency to need to reschedule shooting dates at the last minute. I got each of the principal actors to complete a Doodle poll to register their available days in the July holidays, giving me a clear indication of their availability. I also scheduled back-up dates for each shoot in case something unexpected happened.

A second factor was that rainfall was incorporated into my script. As part of my research and development process, I conducted an experiment to see if I could manufacture a realistic rain effect, but none of these had the desired aesthetic effect, so I decided to try to capture the moment with authentic rainfall. This meant I had to adjust my timeline throughout the shoot, using the Bureau of Meteorology to ascertain a week in advance which days would work best for the scene with rainfall, cross-checking that with my actor's availability.

Mark allocation: 4 marks

For each element discussed:

- 2 marks: An insightful explanation of how the student considered the identified element when planning the timeline of their production process. The response may contain specific examples to support their discussion.
- 1 mark: A general explanation of how the student considered the identified element when planning the timeline of their production process.

Question 2

Sample response

The primary intention of my product, a conventional horror film called *The Cycle*, was to communicate the dangers of the Australian coastline. As a lifesaver, I have witnessed first-hand the drownings that occur in our oceans and wanted to convey the threat our beaches pose to unsuspecting swimmers. In order to do this, I constructed a narrative arc that focused on a supernatural drowning event, whereby a drowning victim emerges from the ocean to claim a victim of her own to take her place. Because I wanted my audience to recognise the ocean as a character, I designed my storyboard to include sweeping landscape pans of the beach at the beginning of each act, and I planned to open and close my film on black with J and L cuts of diegetic ocean ambience. I believed this would clearly establish the importance of the water to the audience, introduce and reinforce the cyclical nature of the narrative, and create a sense that drownings are frequent and dangerous.

Mark allocation: 5 marks

- 5 marks: The student has provided a detailed discussion of the way a media product was designed to achieve a specific intention. The student has set out clear parameters for their success (e.g. conveying a specific message to the audience and constructing a film that effectively fits an intended genre) and given specific and appropriate example/s of how they planned to ensure this success in the production process. Thorough use of appropriate media language is evident in the response.
- 4 marks: The student has provided a clear discussion of the way a media product was designed to achieve a specific intention. The student has set out general parameters for their success and given relevant example/s of how they planned to ensure this success in the production process. Appropriate application of media language is evident in the response.
- 3 marks: The student has provided a general discussion of the way a media product was designed to achieve an intention. The student has set out some parameters for their success and given an example of how they planned to ensure this success in the production process. Some application of media language is evident in the response.
- 2 marks: The student has provided a limited discussion of the way a media product was designed to achieve an intention. The student has referred generally to their intention and given a broad or unrelated example of how they planned to ensure this success in the production process. An attempt to use media language is evident; however, this may be with some inaccuracies.
- 1 mark: The student has provided an incomplete or very limited response that answers some part of the question. Little or no use of media language is evident in the response.

Question 3

Sample response

> In my production plan, I used a written shot list document in conjunction with mock-ups of my photography series, titled *Mermates*, which featured pairs of people in costume and makeup immersed in a pool. To do this, I used my drone camera to take bird's-eye shots of my backyard pool, which was the setting for my photos. Using my shot list, which identified each shot and included a description of my model's body language, I planned out the positions and poses for my subjects and had them act these out while lying on a green bed sheet on the floor. In this way, I was able to quickly superimpose the planned images onto the pool shots to get a visual representation of what I wanted my final images to look like. The process was also helpful in preparing the subjects to be photographed and figuring out which poses were most visually striking so I did not have to take too many alternative shots on the day of the actual shoot.

Mark allocation: 4 marks

- 4 marks: The student has provided a detailed and specific example of how they created written and visual planning documents for a media product. They have made a highly appropriate connection between this example and their ability to plan their product. Effective media language is used in the response.
- 3 marks: The student has provided a clear and specific example of how they created written and/or visual planning documents for a media product. They have made a sound connection between this example and their ability to plan their product. Relevant media language is used in the response.

- 2 marks: The student has provided a general example of how they created written and/or visual planning documents for a media product. They have made some connection between this example and their ability to plan their product. Some media language is used in the response.
- 1 mark: The student has identified a form of a written or visual planning document for a media product. They may or may not have provided some description of how this enabled them to plan their product. Limited or no media language is used in the response.

Question 4

Sample response

> In my product, which was a satirical reality television show called *MasterGardener*, I employed camera techniques and character establishment and development to accurately reflect the stylistic conventions of other reality television programs. In doing so, I aimed to fulfil the expectations of my intended audience, who consider themselves reality television fans, familiar with shows such as *MasterChef* and *The Block*.
>
> Within the narrative, I used character establishment and development to mimic the way reality television programs follow a cast of contestants, cross-cutting between the various conflicts, victories and setbacks experienced by each of them. In the production plan, I developed a character arc for each of my six contestants, which was based around a loose structure of introduction, goals, conflict and eviction/victory. Furthermore, I attempted to establish and develop characters so that they fit the traditional character tropes of reality television, including the cheesy host (Carl), the villain (Terry), the dark horse (Garry) and the crying mess (Cherrie). By giving these characters familiar roles, I aimed to heighten engagement for my audience, who were able to develop narrative possibilities based on how characters following these tropes have fared in other reality television shows; for example, the audience might expect the villain to be evicted following a dramatic conflict with another contestant, or they might expect the host to use dramatic pauses when announcing the winner of the competition.
>
> I also used camera techniques to mimic the aesthetic style of reality television. This included framing individual contestants in a static, medium close-up shot as they delivered their thoughts to the camera, in order to reflect the interview scenario commonly used in reality television shows. I also employed a hand-held camera technique while following contestants around the local hardware store during a shopping challenge, in order to heighten the tension and excitement in the segment and convey the high stakes of the competition. Finally, I combined a low-angle and dirty shot to create the 'hidden camera' effect, commonly used in reality television to convey secrecy as the camera catches a conflict between characters. These techniques enabled me to create a realistic parody of the reality television style, which gave my product authenticity.

Note: This sample response is of a higher level than a typical student response, in order to show the range of detail that can be used to answer the question.

Mark allocation: 6 marks

- 5–6 marks: The student has clearly identified two codes or conventions, and has developed an insightful and detailed response that comprehensively outlines the rationale for employing these in their product, with specific reference to form, product details or intended audience.
- 3–4 marks: The student has identified two codes or conventions, and has developed a clear and competent response that justifies employing these in their product, with reference to form, product details or intended audience.
- 1–2 marks: The student may have identified one or two codes or conventions, but the response is limited or incomplete, and may give only a limited justification for employing these in the product.

Note: Students may be marked at the lower end of each range if they have not discussed each of the two selected codes or conventions in equal depth.

TIP

» **Ensure you refer to a specific audience, such as by identifying their age and/or interests.**

Question 5

Sample response

For my spoof action film *Velocity Rising*, a media process I undertook was educating myself on how to use motion graphics and experimenting with software to elevate the particularly fast-paced scenes of my film. After storyboarding key scenes and identifying where motion graphics would best fit, I watched a range of YouTube tutorials and read guides on how to use Adobe After Effects. These tutorials enabled me to learn basic exercises so I could create custom graphics, typography and animations as well as explore the common pre-made effects like particle simulations. I was then able to insert these effects around my action hero, Jameson Bourned, during pivotal moments of the film.

Marking allocation: 3 marks

- 3 marks: A thoughtful response that clearly discusses a media process the student undertook to develop their narrative. Specific and relevant examples are used to support the discussion. Relevant media language is used in the response.
- 2 marks: A general response that discusses a media process the student undertook to develop their narrative. A relevant example is used. Some media language is used in the response.
- 1 mark: A limited response that attempts to discuss a media process the student undertook to develop their narrative but that may not provide any additional explanation.

Question 6

Sample response

I intended to use the code of sound and the narrative convention of point of view to engage my audience with my horror film production. Sound played an integral role in my horror film to create atmosphere and build tension for the viewers. In my opening scene, I used ambient noise and the diegetic sounds of the environment, such as leaves crunching as the character walked up their driveway and the sound of the floorboard creaking upstairs when they thought they were alone. I utilised non-diegetic music, such as ominous chords and sounds that escalated in rhythm, whenever the main character suspected someone might be in her house. I also employed the use of silence to both emphasise that she was isolated and to set up sudden bursts of sound, further amplifying the jump scares. In tandem with this, I used subjective points of view, alternating between the main protagonist and what she could hear, and the killer who could see her as she makes herself a cup of tea and when she's sitting on the couch choosing a show on Netflix. By controlling the point of view, I was intending to control the audience's visual perspective and guide their attention to specific details and threats within the frame. I aimed to strategically frame my shots to narrow my audience's field of vision and create a sense of claustrophobia and helplessness.

Mark allocation: 5 marks

- 4–5 marks: The student has provided a detailed and insightful discussion of how they intended to use a media code and/or convention to engage their audience. The student has provided specific and relevant examples. Effective media language is used in the response.
- 3 marks: The student has provided a clear and relevant discussion of how they intended to use a media code and/or convention to engage their audience. The student has provided some relevant examples. Relevant media language has been used in the response.
- 2 marks: The student has provided a general discussion of how they intended to use a media code and/or convention to engage their audience and may have provided a basic example. Some media language has been used in the response.
- 1 mark: The student has provided a weak example of how they intended to use a media code and/or convention to engage their audience. Limited or no media language has been used in the response.

Unit 4 | Area of Study 1 Media production

Question 1

Sample response

In the planning process for my short action film, *The Heist*, I was careful to incorporate action genre codes and conventions in my script and storyboard. For example, when storyboarding a chase sequence where my protagonist Bruce Lane was being pursued by his enemy Spike Sin, I made use of conventional camera techniques. I indicated a hand-held effect would be used for the sequence, as well as multiple shots that framed Bruce's face tightly, to show the pressure he was under as he attempted to escape, while cutting away to shots of Sin slowly gaining on him. These shots are seen frequently in action films and served to further my characterisation of the protagonist as a flawed hero – someone who experiences anxiety and emotion in the face of hardship. I was also able to build this element of my narrative into my script by constructing dialogue that demonstrated Bruce's uncertainty in his role as the hero, with ellipses to represent pauses and the use of interjections and fillers such as 'um' and 'ahhh' in his speech to indicate hesitation and nerves. In this way, the codes and conventions I incorporated in my plans reflected both my specific narrative and its genre.

Mark allocation: 5 marks

- 5 marks: A sophisticated discussion of the way the student planned to use one code and one convention to convey meaning, communicate ideas and/or engage audiences in their selected media narrative. Detailed and highly appropriate example/s have been used to highlight the connection between the intended narrative and the selected code and convention. Effective application of media language is evident in the response.
- 4 marks: A competent discussion of the way the student planned to use one code and one convention to convey meaning, communicate ideas and/or engage audiences in their selected media narrative. Specific and relevant example/s have been referenced to highlight the connection between the intended narrative and the selected code and convention. Appropriate application of media language is evident in the response.
- 3 marks: A general discussion of the way the student planned to use one code and one convention in their selected media narrative. Appropriate example/s may have been used to highlight the connection between the intended narrative and the selected code and convention. Some media language is used in the response.
- 2 marks: A limited discussion of the way the student planned to use one code and one convention in their selected media narrative. A limited example may have been used to substantiate the response. An attempt to use media language is present; however, this may contain some inaccuracies.
- 1 mark: A very limited or incomplete discussion of the way the student planned to use a code or convention in their selected media narrative. Some part of the question is answered. Little or no media language is used in the response.

TIP

» This question asks you to refer to your production plan (previously referred to as production design). Be careful not to discuss your completed product, but rather the planning and design process.

Question 2

Sample response

In refining my podcast product, *How to Solve a Murder Mystery*, I made a number of changes in response to feedback. The product, a fictional radio play that experiments with the conventions of true crime podcasts, is intended to enable sufficient suspension of disbelief in the audience so that they might experience genuine fear. However, my initial feedback suggested that my construction of foley was not sufficiently realistic in a scene where a character is stabbed, and this was found to be humorous rather than scary. I recognised the importance of the suspension of disbelief in achieving my intention as it is paramount to engaging an audience effectively. This prompted me to conduct further research into realistic stabbing sounds, and I was able to find increased success by placing a wet flannel over a cabbage and stabbing through the fabric, which was more effective than my initial technique. Furthermore, my family commented that in the second episode my soundtrack competed with an important character monologue, making it difficult for them to focus on the specifics of what the character was saying. As the monologue revealed a clue that would later play an important role in the protagonist solving the mystery, I revised the volume levels and shifted the track so that a softer part of the soundtrack played during the crucial section of the monologue. In my second round of feedback surveys, I saw an increase in the percentage of audience members who felt the ending was satisfying, with one member suggesting that they 'felt more equipped to help solve the mystery' as they had picked up on the clue.

Mark allocation: 6 marks

- 6 marks: A sophisticated discussion of the way undertaking feedback and reflection processes influenced the student's completed media product. Considered references may be made to attempts to appropriately reflect the intention, audience, genre and style, narrative or codes and conventions set out in the production plan. The student has provided two detailed and highly appropriate examples of the alterations or refinements that were made in response to feedback and reflection. Media language is used effectively throughout the response.
- 5 marks: A detailed discussion of the way undertaking feedback and reflection processes influenced the student's completed media product. Appropriate reference may be made to attempts to appropriately reflect the intention, audience, genre and style, narrative or codes and conventions set out in the production plan. The student has provided two specific and appropriate examples of the alterations or refinements that were made in response to feedback and reflection. Appropriate media language is used throughout the response.

- 4 marks: A clear discussion of the way undertaking feedback and reflection processes influenced the student's completed media product. Some reference may be made to attempts to appropriately reflect the intention, audience, genre and style, narrative or codes and conventions set out in the production plan. The student has provided two relevant examples of the alterations or refinements that were made in response to feedback and reflection. Appropriate media language is used in the response.
- 3 marks: A general discussion of the way undertaking feedback and reflection processes influenced the student's completed media product. The student may reference attempts to reflect the intention, audience, genre and style, narrative or codes and conventions set out in the production plan. The student has provided at least one example of the alterations or refinements that were made in response to feedback and reflection. Some media language is used in the response.
- 2 marks: A limited discussion of the way undertaking feedback and reflection processes influenced the student's completed media product. The student may have referred generally to feedback they received and given an unrelated example or a broad example of how they responded to this. An attempt to use media language is evident; however, this may contain inaccuracies.
- 1 mark: An incomplete or very limited response that answers part of the question. Little or no use of media language is evident in the response.

Question 3

Sample response

> The process of creating a production journal gave me the opportunity to narrow down the broad scope of my research. Although I started out exploring the thriller film genre more generally, in my journalling process I realised that the thriller products I was most excited by contained some element of comedy, such as *Mr. & Mrs. Smith* and *A Simple Favour*. This inspired me to refine my production plan to focus on the creation of a film that fits into the comedy thriller subgenre.

Mark allocation: 3 marks

- 3 marks: The student has provided a clear and relevant example of how their written or visual document impacted their production plan. Relevant media language is used in the response.
- 2 marks: The student has provided a general example of how their written or visual document impacted their production plan. Some media language is used in the response.
- 1 mark: The student has identified a limited example of how their written or visual document impacted their production plan. Limited or no media language is used in the response.

Question 4

Sample response

> My media product was a zine called *All Pigeons Are Anarchists* and was aimed at an intended audience of 18- to 24-year-olds from Melbourne who identify politically as socialists. My audience comprises the type of people who listen to underground music, support small local businesses and attend anti-capitalist rallies. This is reflected in the content of my zine, which includes an essay on the issues with Black Friday sales, an interview with a founding member of a local socialist resistance group and a review of the biggest underground drops of 2024 – a collection of niche content that would appeal directly to my delineated group.

Mark allocation: 3 marks

- 3 marks: The student has provided a detailed and considered description of an intended audience. They have clearly related this audience to their media product. Relevant media language is evident in the response.
- 2 marks: The student has provided a general description of an intended audience and made some connection between this and their media product. Some media language is evident in the response.
- 1 mark: The student has provided a limited response that broadly identifies an audience and includes some reference to a media product. Limited or no media language is evident in the response.

TIP

» **Remember, the examiners are unaware of your media production plan and your product, so ensure you provide the context of your work.**

Question 5

Sample response

> My media narrative centred around the relationship between two primary school-aged children who see each other as associates in the classroom but rivals on the playground. Because this meant most of my dialogue and acting would be performed by young actors, I ensured my script and storyboard reflected their needs. Instead of sketching images for my storyboard, I took photos of my actors performing each required action, movement and facial expression so that they would have the opportunity to run through the performance before filming and could refer back to the images to jog their memory if needed. I also kept my script simple and included the basic phonetic spelling of words that I thought might be tricky for my actors to pronounce.

Mark allocation: 4 marks

- 4 marks: The student has provided a detailed and insightful discussion of how they applied production processes appropriate to their form or narrative. They have made clear connections between the narrative and the way they used production processes to benefit the narrative. Effective media language is used in the response.
- 3 marks: The student has provided a clear and relevant discussion of how they applied production processes appropriate to their form or narrative. They have made sound connections between the narrative and the way they used production processes to benefit the narrative. Relevant media language is used in the response.
- 2 marks: The student has provided a general discussion of how they applied production processes appropriate to their form or narrative. They have made some connections between the narrative and the way they used production processes to benefit the narrative. Some media language is used in the response.
- 1 mark: The student has provided an incomplete or very limited response that answers some part of the question. Little or no use of media language is evident in the response.

Note: If the student has opted to discuss a media form rather than a narrative, the response may be slightly more general in nature but should otherwise be of the same standard.

Question 6

Sample response

One refinement I made to my graphic novel was changing the product from greyscale to colour. I intended for my graphic novel to contribute to normalising LGBTQIA+ relationships while fulfilling conventions of the magic realism genre. During the pre-production phase of my graphic novel, I created a greyscale product because I believed this would fit within the time constraints while still meeting the conventions of the form. However, I was able to use time more effectively than anticipated in the production process. In addition, I realised my graphic novel would be better suited to a limited colour palette in order to bring to life some of the magic and romantic themes. After colouring my sketches, I printed one page of the novel in greyscale and one in colour and gave them to members of my intended audience for feedback. They unanimously affirmed my decision to use colour, suggesting that it was a better way to convey warmth and affection between the protagonists, as well as to make my product more engaging.

Note: Refinements you may discuss include: colour correction, changes to dialogue, changes to casting, additional scenes or deleted scenes, or changes in score or soundtrack.

Mark allocation: 5 marks

- 4–5 marks: The student has developed a detailed and insightful analysis of how the selected refinement enabled them to achieve an intention for their media product. The student has likely referred to the feedback processes and used these to justify the effectiveness of this refinement. Effective media language is used in the response.
- 3 marks: The student has provided a clear and relevant analysis of how the selected refinement enabled them to achieve an intention for their media product. They may have referred to the feedback processes implemented in post-production. Relevant media language is used in the response.
- 2 marks: The student has provided a general explanation of how the selected refinement enabled them to achieve part of their intention for their media product. Some media language is used in the response.
- 1 mark: The student has provided a limited description of the selected refinement. They may not have linked this to their intention. Limited or no media language is used in the response.

TIP

» **When considering your refinement, think about the feedback you received and how this helped you to shape your product.**

Question 7

Sample response

> While working on the production of my photographic series *Baby Meets World*, I made two significant refinements to the technologies and processes I was using. The first was to go from using a DSLR camera to shooting on my iPhone XS. The factor that led to this refinement was a scheduling conflict with another student, but in the end using my iPhone had a positive outcome. Setting up each shot manually on the DSLR was a time-consuming and frustrating process, particularly when the subject of my series – my ten-month-old cousin – moved constantly and had a limited capacity for following instructions. Using portrait mode on my iPhone allowed me to capture shots far more quickly, and then alter the depth control of my shots easily using the in-built software. A second refinement I made was switching from using Adobe Photoshop to Adobe Lightroom. The factor that influenced this decision was that I was finding it difficult to maintain consistency in the tone and colour of my shots across the series, and it was suggested to me that Lightroom allows creators to create and apply a preset, eliminating the frustrating process of adjusting levels in every shot.

Mark allocation: 5 marks

- 5 marks: The student has developed a detailed and insightful discussion of how they came to make refinements to the materials, technologies and/or processes that they used in the creation of their media product. The student has provided two examples of factors that led to these refinements, which may include things like feedback from peers or unexpected complications that arose in the production process, and discussed them equally. Effective media language is used in the response.
- 4 marks: The student has developed a thorough and relevant discussion of how they came to make refinements to the materials, technologies and/or processes that they used in the creation of their media product. The student has provided two examples of factors that led to these refinements and discussed them equally. Effective media language is used in the response.
- 3 marks: The student has provided a clear and relevant discussion of how they came to make refinements to the materials, technologies and/or processes that they used in the creation of their media product. The student has provided two examples of factors that led to these refinements, although one may have been discussed in more detail than the other. Appropriate media language is used in the response.
- 2 marks: The student has outlined two factors that led to the refinement of the materials, technologies and/or processes that they used in the creation of their media product OR the student has provided a basic discussion of how they came to make these refinements, with reference to at least one factor. Some media language is used in the response.
- 1 mark: Student has provided a limited description of a factor that led to refinement. They may not have linked this to their media product. Limited or no media language is used in the response.

TIP

» **Make sure you discuss each factor in equal depth.**

Question 8

Sample response

> During the feedback process, my audience members were able to pinpoint a moment in the film where my animation needed refinement. One viewer pointed out that when my protagonist jumped over a puddle, he did so without the full range of movements you would see in a real human jump. Another viewer supported this view, and I was prompted to go back and add a deeper crouch prior to my character's take-off and a more realistic landing stance before the character straightened and kept walking. However, the feedback process also introduced complications, as not all my audience members agreed on other aspects. For example, I had been considering changing the music track I had placed at the end of my film, as I was not sure it evoked the bittersweet mood I was aiming for. Feedback from my surveys suggested that half of the audience members felt the new track was suitable for the scene, but the other half had mixed responses, with some believing the track did not elicit a sense of underlying sadness. To resolve this feedback, I slowed down the tempo of my track and added 7ths to my chord progression to build emotional complexity.

Mark allocation: 5 marks

- 5 marks: The student has constructed a comprehensive evaluation of how the reflection or feedback process enabled or hindered the refinement and resolution of a media product. Detailed and relevant examples relating to a media product have been provided, and these are used to demonstrate the application and effectiveness of the reflection or feedback process. Highly appropriate media language is evident in the response.
- 4 marks: The student has constructed a clear evaluation of how the reflection or feedback process enabled or hindered the refinement and resolution of a media product. Specific and relevant examples relating to a media product have been provided, and these are used to demonstrate the application and effectiveness of the reflection or feedback process. Appropriate media language is evident in the response.
- 3 marks: The student has provided a general discussion of the reflection or feedback process and attempted to evaluate how this enabled or hindered the refinement and resolution of a media product. Broad examples relating to a media product have been used to show the application and effectiveness of the reflection or feedback process. Relevant media language is evident in the response.
- 2 marks: The student has identified a reflection or feedback process and outlined how the process identified was used to refine or resolve their product OR the student has provided a basic discussion of how they came to make refinements to their product. Little or no attempt has been made to evaluate the reflection or feedback process. Some media language is evident in the response.
- 1 mark: The student has identified a reflection or feedback process and has provided some description of how they refined or resolved their media product. Limited or no media language is evident in the response.

Unit 4 | Area of Study 2 Agency and control in the media Section A

Question 1

Sample response

The globalisation of the media has had a significant impact on the media products Australian audiences are able to consume, and how they are able to consume them. Diverse networks of global media users are working to share and translate products from different countries for Australian audiences. An example was seen in the immense cult popularity of Norwegian transmedia show *Skam*, which developed an international following through the social networking website Tumblr. Although the show itself was entirely produced in Norwegian, communities of Australian, American and British teens worked alongside their Norwegian Tumblr friends to get English translations and subtitles for every segment of the show, and these were published on Tumblr within hours of each episode's release. In this way, Australian audiences were able to participate in the global phenomenon very quickly, despite language and time-zone barriers.

Mark allocation: 3 marks

- 3 marks: The student has clearly and insightfully explained one way in which globalisation has impacted how Australian audiences consume media products. The response may include a relevant example.
- 2 marks: The student has competently outlined one way in which globalisation has impacted how Australian audiences consume media products, and may have included a limited example.
- 1 mark: The student has identified an impact of globalisation, but the response may be limited or incomplete, without a relevant link to Australian audiences.

Question 2

Sample response

Media theorists have been attempting to explain the nature and extent of media communication for many years, and in doing so have constructed many conflicting theories relating to the roles of the media and audiences. Traditional theories and models, such as the Shannon and Weaver model of communication or the Hypodermic Needle model, focus on a one-way line of communication from the media to its audience. However, the contemporary media landscape, with its vast array of platforms, forms and products, cannot be reduced to such simplistic hypotheses. For example, the use of social media platforms such as X (formerly Twitter), Tumblr, Facebook and Instagram by both media creators and consumers means there is an open line of communication between fans and the creators of their favourite products. In turn, this has seen the consumers of media products find increasing agency within the media landscape. For example, after the titular character of the BBC television series *Sherlock* was killed off at the end of the second season, fans took to social media to share their elaborate theories about how Holmes had faked his own death. These made their way back to the show's creators, Mark Gatiss and Steven Moffat, and, subsequently, the first episode of the third season paid fan service to these theories, building a plot that both addressed and drew from these conspiratorial musings. The fact that fans did not simply accept Holmes' death as fact, and the influence of this on the content of the next season, contradicts traditional beliefs about the media having a direct and one-sided impact on audiences, suggesting instead that the modern relationship between the media and its audience is open and fluid.

Mark allocation: 5 marks

- 4–5 marks: The student has written a detailed and sophisticated response, demonstrating a thorough understanding of the relationship between the media and its audience as it exists in the contemporary media landscape, while also providing a discussion of how this conflicts with or develops earlier beliefs about the relationship. The student may have provided an insightful and relevant example to support their response, and has used appropriate media language throughout.
- 2–3 marks: The student has written a competent response, demonstrating a sound understanding of the relationship between the media and its audience as it exists in the contemporary media landscape, while also providing some discussion of how this conflicts with or develops earlier beliefs about the relationship. The student may have provided a broad or somewhat relevant example to support their response and has used some media language.
- 1 mark: The student has written a limited or incomplete response that attempts to convey some understanding of the relationship between the media and its audience.

Question 3

Sample response

The provided image suggests that the co-dependent relationship that exists between social media and advertising is necessary if both halves of the dichotomy are to function effectively. This relationship can be seen to cause significant ethical and legal issues in modern society, as the personal content produced by users of social media is being used to the financial benefit of corporations, often without the explicit permission of the content creators or audiences.

Facebook users will by now be aware that their data is used by the company to target them with specific advertising based on their demographic. This monetisation of personal data creates an ethical issue as, despite the fact that users are technically aware that it is occurring, having had to agree to Facebook's terms and conditions upon signing up to the service, they are not necessarily aware of when and how this data will be used to target them. For example, in 2011, Procter and Gamble produced the 'Celebrate Life' campaign to advertise Pepto-Bismol after discovering that the product was being widely discussed on Facebook on Saturday and Sunday mornings. The company switched their attention from television advertising to Facebook advertising, and saw an 11 per cent gain in their share value over the next year. This could be seen as ethically questionable as audiences were using their Facebook profiles to share their personal woes while, unbeknown to them, a multinational manufacturer was using this data to increase their market value.

The Australian Association of National Advertisers (AANA) has also acknowledged the potential ethical issues inherent in social media marketing. In March 2017, they established a code that encourages social media influencers to label their posts with #ad or #sponsored in order to clearly communicate to their audiences that the content has been paid for by brands. This aimed to prevent conduct such as that demonstrated by South Australia Tourism in 2012 with their Kangaroo Island campaign, in which they offered $750 to high profile celebrities for an 'organic' tweet about Kangaroo Island. This underhanded marketing technique sought to attract tourists by relying on the recommendation of influencers who had been paid to endorse the product. The change in regulatory code acknowledges the need to reduce deception in social media advertising and make it more immediately obvious to consumers when they are viewing sponsored recommendations from influencers, allowing them to make conscious decisions about their reception of sponsored content.

Note: This sample response is of a higher level than a typical student response, in order to show the range of detail that can be used to answer the question.

Mark allocation: 6 marks

- 5–6 marks: The student has developed a considered discussion about how the co-dependence of social media and advertising poses an ethical or legal issue, particularly with reference to production, distribution, consumption and/or reception. The response has been supported with specific and relevant examples that convey a sophisticated level of understanding as to how this issue may appear in the contemporary media landscape. The student has employed a wide range of appropriate media language in their response.

- 3–4 marks: The student has developed a competent discussion about how the co-dependence of social media and advertising poses an ethical or legal issue, and has referenced production, distribution, consumption and/or reception. The response has been supported with examples that convey a sound level of understanding as to how this issue may appear in the contemporary media landscape. The student has employed some appropriate media language in their response.
- 1–2 marks: The student has developed a limited or incomplete discussion about how the relationship between social media and advertising poses an ethical or legal issue. This may be simplistic or fail to reference production, distribution, consumption and/or reception. The student may have employed some limited media language in their response.

TIP

» **You do not necessarily need to refer to communication theories in response to this question, but some of these (such as Two-Step Flow theory or Filter Bubble theory) may be useful in illustrating your point.**

Question 4

Sample response

One legal issue that relates to the production and distribution of user-generated content is the ease with which modern media producers may create content containing other people and disseminate it to large audiences without their permission. The development of social media platforms that rely on user-generated content, such as Instagram, Facebook and Snapchat, has led to a number of instances where such content has been created and distributed. The unregulated upload of content can have serious ramifications for the privacy of individuals, and may result in legal penalties. For example, in 2017, model Dani Mathers was found guilty of invasion of privacy after using her phone to take a photo of an elderly woman in her gym change room and sharing it with her Snapchat followers.

Mark allocation: 4 marks

- 4 marks: The student has constructed a detailed and sophisticated response that demonstrates an insightful understanding of the relationship between user-generated content and one legal or ethical issue. The student has supported their answer with a specific example. Highly effective use of appropriate media language is evident in the response.
- 3 marks: The student has constructed a clear response that demonstrates a sound understanding of the relationship between user-generated content and one legal or ethical issue. The student has supported their answer with a clear and relevant example. Effective use of appropriate media language is evident in the response.
- 2 marks: The student has constructed a response that demonstrates a basic understanding of the relationship between user-generated content and one legal or ethical issue. The student has supported their response with an example, but this may be general in nature. Some use of appropriate media language is evident in the response.

- 1 mark: The student has constructed a limited response that addresses part of the question or is incomplete. The student may simply have identified a legal or ethical issue and made a broad statement about its relationship to modern media technologies. Little or no use of appropriate media language is evident in the response.

Question 5

Sample response

> The relationship between the media and audiences has changed as a result of globalisation and new developments in technology. Thus, the way in which commercial content is produced and distributed has changed significantly. The first image reflects traditional forms of advertising, detailing goods and services that are available, as seen in the classifieds section of print media such as newspapers. This form of advertising originated before the broadcast era and reflects the beliefs of early media theorists that audiences received content somewhat passively. Another example from an earlier era includes the Uncle Sam 'I Want You' army recruitment poster. However, in the digital age, there have been many developments in how advertising can appear. The advent of the internet has given audiences significant control over the content they consume, and social media platforms such as Facebook and Instagram have given rise to the new practice of sponsored content, or 'spon con'. The second image reflects this new development, whereby social media users can be paid by companies to promote their goods and services. There has been criticism of the ethics of such practices. For instance, actress Jameela Jamil condemned the Kardashian family for using their Instagram accounts to promote Fit Tea, a weight-loss tea product, in a series of sponsored posts. Jamil wrote 'When will these women who are covered in plastic surgery stop telling their followers to drink a laxative to look like them?' In doing so, Jamil highlighted how the use of advertising on social media platforms creates further potential for companies to cross ethical boundaries.

Mark allocation: 6 marks

- 6 marks: The student has provided a sophisticated discussion of the way commercial content has evolved over time, with specific, insightful and balanced reference to each image. There is a highly relevant discussion of the legal and/or ethical issues that changes to commercial content may have caused. Specific and highly appropriate examples have been used to substantiate discussion. Effective application of media language is evident in the response.
- 5 marks: The student has provided a detailed discussion of the way commercial content has evolved over time, with highly appropriate and balanced reference to each image. There is a thorough discussion of the legal and/or ethical issues that changes to commercial content may have caused. Specific examples have been used to substantiate discussion. Thorough use of appropriate media language is evident in the response.

- 4 marks: The student has provided a clear discussion of the way commercial content has evolved over time, with highly appropriate reference to each image. There is an appropriate discussion of the legal and/or ethical issues that changes to commercial content may have caused. Relevant examples have been used to substantiate discussion. Appropriate application of media language is evident in the response.
- 3 marks: The student has provided a general discussion of the way commercial content has evolved over time, with reference to the image/s. There is some understanding of the legal and/or ethical issues that changes to commercial content may have caused. Basic examples have been used to substantiate discussion. Some application of media language is evident in the response.
- 2 marks: The student has provided a limited discussion of the way commercial content has evolved over time, which has limited relevance to the image/s. There is a basic understanding of the legal and/or ethical issues that changes to commercial content may have caused. Limited or general examples may have been used as part of the response. An attempt to use media language is evident; however, this may be with some inaccuracies.
- 1 mark: The student has provided an incomplete or very limited response that answers part of the question. Little or no use of media language is evident in the response.

Question 6

Sample response

> The advent of social media has presented global media institutions with opportunities to directly exert control over their audiences through the manipulation of content and advertising. In 2014, users of the globalised media institution Facebook were shocked to learn the media giant had been conducting secret experiments on its users to learn how to impact their moods. As part of a study with the University of California and Cornell University, Facebook selectively altered the newsfeed content of around 689 000 users to see if the concept of 'emotional contagion' could be created. The study found that when users were presented with more positive material, they produced positive material themselves. On the other hand, if their newsfeeds contained more negative content, they produced negative content. While the study may not appear sinister, it has since been suggested that Facebook's interest in this area of research could point to more questionable intentions. Jim Sheridan, who was a British MP at the time, condemned the institution, stating that 'they are manipulating material from people's personal lives and I am worried about the ability of Facebook and others to manipulate people's thoughts in politics or other areas'.

Mark allocation: 5 marks

- 5 marks: The student has provided a sophisticated discussion of the way a clearly identified globalised media institution (e.g. Facebook, Apple, Google, Samsung, Instagram) or individual has attempted to exert control over a specific audience. A detailed and highly appropriate example has been used to substantiate the response. Effective application of media language is evident in the response.

- 4 marks: The student has provided a competent discussion of the way a clearly identified globalised media institution or individual has attempted to exert control over a specific audience. A detailed and relevant example has been used to substantiate the response. Appropriate application of media language is evident in the response.
- 3 marks: The student has provided a general discussion of the way a globalised media institution or an individual has attempted to exert control over an audience. The student has used a general example to substantiate the response. Some application of media language is evident in the response.
- 2 marks: The student has provided a limited discussion of the way a globalised media institution or an individual has attempted to exert control over an audience. A limited example may have been used to substantiate the response. An attempt to use media language is evident; however, this may be with some inaccuracies.
- 1 mark: The student has provided a very limited or incomplete discussion of the way a globalised media institution or an individual has attempted to exert control over a loosely defined audience. Some part of the question is answered. Little or no use of media language is evident in the response.

Question 7

Sample response

> Australia's regulatory bodies have struggled to maintain control over the media landscape because globalisation and the internet have provided limitless ways for audiences to access media content. While bodies such as Ad Standards, the National Classification Scheme and Free TV Australia were previously able to monitor Australian media content quite effectively, they no longer have complete jurisdiction over certain streaming and social media services. This challenge came to the fore when streaming service Netflix released the teen drama *13 Reasons Why* in 2017. The program, which contained explicit depictions of suicide, did not go through the traditional forms of regulation. Although the Turnbull government had, at the time of its release, begun planning for a self-regulation classification tool for Netflix, this had not yet come into action and the show's content sparked a moral panic in Australia. By the time the second season of *13 Reasons Why* was released in Australia, the show contained a content warning (read by cast members) that played before the first episode as well as subsequent episodes that contained violence or gun use. Although this was a significant improvement in Netflix's operations, Australia's regulatory bodies must find ways to manage streaming services as they emerge.

Mark allocation: 5 marks

- 5 marks: The student has provided a sophisticated discussion of a clearly identified challenge facing Australia's regulatory bodies as a result of globalisation and contemporary media practices (e.g. the rise of streaming services or social media). The discussion is substantiated with a detailed and highly appropriate example. Effective application of media language is evident in the response.
- 4 marks: The student has provided a competent discussion of a clearly identified challenge facing Australia's regulatory bodies as a result of globalisation and contemporary media practices. The discussion is substantiated with a detailed and relevant example. Appropriate application of media language is evident in the response.

- 3 marks: The student has provided a general discussion of a clearly identified challenge facing Australia's regulatory bodies as a result of globalisation and contemporary media practices. The student has used a general example to substantiate the response. Some application of media language is evident in the response.
- 2 marks: The student has provided a limited response that identifies a challenge faced by regulatory bodies and relates this to globalisation and contemporary media practices. Limited or no example has been used to substantiate the response. An attempt to use media language is evident; however, this may be with some inaccuracies.
- 1 mark: The student has provided a very limited or incomplete response that shows little or no understanding of a challenge faced by regulatory bodies as a result of globalisation and contemporary media practices. Part of the question is answered. Little or no use of media language is evident in the response.

TIP

» **This question asks you to discuss Australia's regulatory bodies, so ensure that your answer is specific to Australia.**

Question 8

Sample response

The increasingly broad media landscape is a challenge to regulators. For example, globalisation of the media has made it difficult for governments to regulate the media in their jurisdiction, which means audiences may engage with content that does not meet Australia's regulatory standards. An example of this is Ad Standards' inability to regulate advertising on platforms such as Instagram. While Ad Standards has codes of conduct for advertising aimed at children, for example, requiring that ads 'accurately represent the advertised product in a manner that is clearly understood by children', such advertising codes had not previously been enforced by Instagram. This allowed influencers such as the Kardashian family to consistently advertise misleading weight-loss products, such as Fit Tea, to their wide, and often young, audiences, without disclosing their diet and exercise regimes or use of plastic surgery procedures to obtain weight-loss results. As a result of situations such as this, in 2019, Instagram brought in a policy to ensure users under the age of 18 were not able to see weight-loss advertisements.

Mark allocation: 4 marks

- 4 marks: A sophisticated explanation of at least one issue or challenge that may arise in media regulation. The response is substantiated with a detailed and highly appropriate example. Effective media language is used throughout the response.
- 3 marks: A competent explanation of at least one issue or challenge that may arise in media regulation. The response is substantiated with a specific and relevant example. Appropriate media language is used in the response.
- 2 marks: A general explanation of one issue or challenge that may arise in media regulation. The student has used a general example to substantiate the response. Some media language is used in the response.

- 1 mark: A very limited or incomplete response that shows basic understanding of a challenge or issue faced by regulatory bodies. Little or no media language is used in the response.

TIP

» **It may help to focus on the actions of a specific Australian regulatory body in your response.**

Question 9

Sample response

The harvesting and sale of personal information has contributed to other issues surrounding a loss of privacy and breaches of the democratic process. This was seen in the Cambridge Analytica scandal, which took advantage of the way audiences consume media products in order to manipulate their reception of other products. In 2014 and 2015, an online survey called 'This Is Your Digital Life' was distributed on Facebook, collecting personal data from 270 000 participants and their Facebook friends. This data was passed to Cambridge Analytica, which used it to target users with tailored political advertising during the 2016 US presidential election. This was acknowledged globally as having been a major breach in privacy, despite the survey participants having agreed to the data harvesting in the Terms and Conditions. This sparked discussion around the ethics of Terms and Conditions. A 2012 study by Carnegie Mellon University found that the average person would need 76 days to read through the privacy policies they view each year. It's been suggested that it is unreasonable for companies to influence democratic elections by manipulating users who have unknowingly contributed to a database of information. Therefore, companies like Cambridge Analytica are altering the potential reception of media products by capitalising on the consumption habits of audiences.

Mark allocation: 5 marks

- 5 marks: The student has constructed a detailed and sophisticated response that demonstrates an insightful understanding of the relationship between the harvesting and sale of personal information and one legal and/or ethical issue that may arise from this development. In their response, they have thoughtfully related their discussion to two of the required dot points. The student may have supported their answer with a specific and detailed example. Highly effective use of appropriate media language is evident in the response.
- 4 marks: The student has constructed a competent response that demonstrates a considered understanding of the relationship between the harvesting and sale of personal information and one legal and/or ethical issue that may arise from this development. In their response, they have appropriately related their discussion to two of the required dot points. The student may have supported their answer with a relevant example. Highly appropriate use of relevant media language is evident in the response.

- 3 marks: The student has constructed a clear response that demonstrates an understanding of the relationship between the harvesting and sale of personal information and one legal and/or ethical issue that may arise from this development. In their response, they have related their discussion to two of the required dot points. The student may have supported their answer with an example. Effective use of media language is evident in the response.
- 2 marks: The student has constructed a response that demonstrates a basic understanding of the relationship between the harvesting and sale of personal information and one legal and/or ethical issue that may arise from this development. They have related their response to at least one of the provided dot points. Some use of appropriate media language is evident in the response.
- 1 mark: The student has constructed a limited response that addresses some part of the question but may be incomplete. The student may simply have identified a legal or ethical issue and made a broad statement about its relationship to modern media technologies. Little or no use of appropriate media language is evident in the response.

Question 10a.

Sample response

One issue or challenge relating to regulation and control of the media is the creation and dissemination of harmful content.

Mark allocation: 1 mark

- 1 mark: An appropriate issue or challenge relating to regulation and control of the media has been identified.

Question 10b.

Sample response

The creation and dissemination of harmful content has become an ongoing challenge in media regulation, particularly on social media platforms such as Facebook, TikTok, Instagram and X (formerly known as Twitter). Harmful content can be described as any content that can cause an individual harm or distress. It can include misinformation or disinformation, which can lead to a lack of trust in media institutions, as well as content that aims to cause fear, uncertainty or doubt, and discrimination, such as hate speech targeting social, religious or political groups.

One of the biggest issues with harmful content on social media is the difficulty of regulating user-generated content, particularly content that can be uploaded and shared very quickly, such as through livestreaming. In April 2024, a livestream of a service at an Assyrian church, Christ the Good Shepherd, showed a 16-year-old boy attack and stab a priest and a bishop. The graphic video of the attack was streamed and shared, which caused hundreds of people to go to the church and clash with police. A member of the Assyrian community commented that people were reacting to the content spread on social media, stating 'there were many inflammatory posts making the rounds, people advocating for violence', indicating the widespread and dangerous impact of harmful content being created and disseminated.

Platforms such as Facebook set their own guidelines when it comes to regulation and place much of the responsibility on the user, relying on users to report issues that breach their community standards. Facebook also uses artificial intelligence to detect and block harmful content, and users can be temporarily or permanently banned if they breach the rules. However, users can get around this by creating multiple accounts, showing the challenges faced by regulatory bodies or platforms.

Mark allocation: 4 marks

- 4 marks: A thoughtful and detailed analysis that explains the issue or challenge mentioned in **part a.** with reference to how regulatory bodies or media platforms manage or regulate the media. The student may use a specific example to substantiate their analysis. Highly appropriate media language is used in the response.
- 3 marks: A clear analysis that explains the issue or challenge mentioned in **part a.** with reference to how regulatory bodies or media platforms manage or regulate the media. The student may use an example to substantiate their analysis. Relevant media language is used in the response.
- 2 marks: A general response that explains the issue or challenge mentioned in **part a.** with reference to how regulatory bodies or media platforms manage or regulate the media. Some media language is used in the response.
- 1 mark: A limited response that demonstrates a basic understanding of the issue or challenge mentioned in **part a.** with reference to how regulatory bodies or media platforms manage or regulate the media. Limited or no media language is used in the response.

Question 11

Sample response

The media landscape is dynamic and constantly changing. Two ways the relationship between the media and its audience has changed over time are the speed of the feedback loop between audience and producer, and the role of the audience, who have shifted from being limited to being spectators to participating in content creation and production.

The feedback loop between the media and its audience has always existed, but audience feedback was limited and responding to it took time. For example, fans of television shows in the mid-twentieth century would write feedback letters to a network, such as when audiences wrote letters to *I Love Lucy* after the show's initial airing regarding its portrayal of interracial marriage. However, in the modern sphere, the media responds actively to audiences, who use social networks to voice collective opinions and see swift results. An example of this was the #savethe99 efforts of fans to get *Brooklyn 99* picked up by another network after it was cancelled by Fox. Twenty-four hours after it had been cancelled, the show was picked up by NBC, suggesting that the media now responds to audiences in real time.

Another change in the relationship can be seen in the way audiences have crossed over from being observers to being creators through new media. While the boundary between the media and audiences was clearly established in the broadcast era, such lines have been blurred as audiences use their smartphones and online platforms such as YouTube, Instagram and TikTok to create and distribute their own content. This has made it difficult to distinguish between creators and audiences, and has given rise to the term 'influencers', the new breed of creator/audience hybrid consumers who are significantly changing the media landscape.

Mark allocation: 6 marks

- 6 marks: The student has outlined two highly appropriate ways the relationship between the media and its audience has changed over time. The response explains in a considered manner how modern technologies and media processes have impacted this relationship, and conveys a sophisticated understanding of the ways the media and audiences interact. Highly appropriate media language has been used in the response.
- 5 marks: The student has outlined two relevant ways the relationship between the media and its audience has changed over time. The response explains in a competent manner how modern technologies and media processes have impacted this relationship and conveys a considered understanding of the ways the media and audiences interact. Thorough application of media language is evident in the response.
- 4 marks: The student has outlined two general ways the relationship between the media and its audience has changed over time. The response explains in a clear manner how the modern media landscape differs to the traditional media landscape. Appropriate application of media language is evident in the response.
- 3 marks: The student has outlined at least one relevant way the relationship between the media and its audience has changed over time. The response attempts to explain how the modern media landscape differs to the traditional media landscape. Some application of media language is evident in the response.
- 2 marks: The student has outlined at least one general way the relationship between the media and its audience has changed over time. The response may attempt to explain how the modern media landscape differs to the traditional media landscape. Limited application of media language is evident in the response.
- 1 mark: An incomplete or very limited response that answers part of the question. Little or no use of media language is evident in the response.

TIP

» **Be sure to consider both the traditional and modern media landscapes in your response.**

Question 12

Sample response

> It is thought that the release of the Netflix show *The Queen's Gambit* in October 2020 led to a significant increase in the purchase of chess sets. The *New York Times* reported the phenomenon in Marie Fazio's article '"*The Queen's Gambit*" Sends Chess Set Sales Soaring' (23 November 2020), in which Fazio outlines the way the show, about a female chess prodigy and her meteoric rise within the world of chess, seemingly influenced audiences to purchase chess sets and learn the game. Between the show's premiere and the article's publication, eBay recorded a 215 per cent increase in the sale of chess sets, and noted that wooden sets, such as those used in the drama, were selling nine times faster than sets made of other materials. Similarly, toy company Goliath Games reported that their own chess set sales were up 1000 per cent compared with the same time in 2019. These statistics seem to imply that the show has had a meaningful influence on its audiences. The connection can also be reasonably justified as a fandom response, rather than any deliberate attempt by the show's creators or Netflix to boost chess sales.

Mark allocation: 4 marks

- 4 marks: The student has constructed a detailed response that demonstrates an insightful understanding of how the media is thought to exert influence. The student has supported their answer with a specific and detailed example. Highly effective use of appropriate media language is evident in the response.
- 3 marks: The student has constructed a clear response that demonstrates a sound understanding of how the media can exert influence. The student has supported their answer with a clear and relevant example. Effective use of appropriate media language is evident in the response.
- 2 marks: The student has constructed a response that demonstrates a basic understanding of how the media can exert influence. The student may have supported their response with an example, but this may be general in nature. Some use of appropriate media language is evident in the response.
- 1 mark: The student has constructed a limited response that addresses some part of the question but may be incomplete. The student may have listed an example of where the media was thought to have exerted influence, with limited or no discussion. Little or no use of appropriate media language is evident in the response.

Question 13

Sample response

> The modern media landscape has changed significantly since the early days of mass media, and so too has the relationship between media and audiences. In the contemporary context, media products are under increasing pressure to be immediate and responsive to global events, and to capture the attention of a generation of media users who expect to be able to consume a greater volume of media products in a shorter time period. These changes can be seen in the way that individuals around the world have taken to using the social media application TikTok. Users of the video-sharing software frequently repurpose original content to create new content that is relevant to more recent situations, which follows the trend of meme creation and distribution that is a hallmark of the modern media landscape. An example of this is the TikTok content created by users as the year 2020, which has become renowned for its global challenges and political tensions, drew to a close. In the lead-up to 1 January 2021, users began creating humorous expressions of their desire to leave 2020 behind, such as user @taylor_reigns, whose 16-second TikTok of her dancing joyfully to a Chris Brown song down a superimposed image of Elm Street, with the caption 'Walk down this hall or repeat 2020', was promoted on TikTok's official Instagram feed. The video itself borrows elements from other videos following the trend, which use the same premise, song and image to comment on other situations that are commonly considered undesirable, like 'returning to your ex'. TikTok users' creation of such short-length videos with repurposed content and relevance to cultural events is a clear example of how contemporary media use reflects the changing relationship between media and audiences.

Mark allocation: 6 marks

- 6 marks: A sophisticated exploration of the ways the changing relationship between the media and audiences is evident in the way that individuals use media. Specific and highly appropriate examples have been used to substantiate discussion. Effective application of media language is evident in the response.
- 5 marks: A detailed exploration of the ways the changing relationship between the media and audiences is evident in the way that individuals use media. Specific examples have been used to substantiate discussion. Thorough use of appropriate media language is evident in the response.
- 4 marks: A clear exploration of the ways the changing relationship between the media and audiences is evident in the way that individuals use media. Relevant examples may have been used to substantiate discussion. Appropriate application of media language is evident in the response.
- 3 marks: A general exploration of the ways the changing relationship between the media and audiences is evident in the way that individuals use media. Basic examples may have been used to substantiate discussion. Some application of media language is evident in the response.
- 2 marks: A limited response that addresses how the changing relationship between the media and audiences is evident in the way that individuals use media. Limited or general examples may have been used as part of the response. An attempt to use media language is evident; however, this may be with some inaccuracies.
- 1 mark: An incomplete or very limited response that answers some part of the question. Little or no use of media language is evident in the response.

Question 14

Sample response

> In its attempts to regulate media use by Australian citizens, the Australian Government has come up against many challenges. One challenge it has faced is its inability to manage misinformation spreading on social media networks about COVID-19. From the beginning of the pandemic, myths surrounding causes, treatments and vaccinations were ubiquitous across X (formerly known as Twitter), Instagram and Facebook, and with much of the content coming from global users outside of the Australian Government's jurisdiction, regulation fell into the hands of the social media platforms and their codes of conduct. Australians were able to consume this content and perpetuate the incorrect information themselves. In an attempt to combat this, the Australian Government set up their 'COVID-19 Mythbusting' webpage, on which they highlighted 20 common myths about the virus by including screenshots of the myths as they have appeared on social media, before providing correct information and links to trustworthy sources for each. This attempt at regulation was limited in its efficacy, as the page itself was on the government's website, so users needed to seek it out in order to benefit from the resource.

Mark allocation: 5 marks

- 5 marks: A sophisticated discussion of one issue that has challenged the Australian Government's ability to manage or regulate media use. A detailed and highly appropriate example has been used to substantiate the response. Effective application of media language is evident in the response.
- 4 marks: A competent discussion of one issue that has challenged the Australian Government's ability to manage or regulate media use. A detailed and relevant example has most likely been used to substantiate the response. Appropriate application of media language is evident in the response.
- 3 marks: A general discussion of one issue that has challenged the Australian Government's ability to manage or regulate media use. Student may have used a general example to substantiate the response. Some application of media language is evident in the response.
- 2 marks: A basic discussion of one issue that has challenged the Australian Government's ability to manage or regulate media use. A limited example may have been used to substantiate the response. An attempt to use media language is evident; however, this may be with some inaccuracies.
- 1 mark: A very limited or incomplete discussion of an issue in regulation. The student may not have referenced the Australian Government in their response. Some part of the question is answered. Little or no use of media language is evident in the response.

TIP

» **Make sure you use a specific example to support your response.**

Question 15

Sample response

Although the media was traditionally thought to exert power over audiences in an unbalanced relationship, in the contemporary media landscape, the agency of both the media and audiences is acknowledged. While the media maintains power as the creator and distributor of content sites and applications, audiences can shape content through selection and omission and an extraordinarily fast feedback loop. For media companies to continue making the money that gives them their agency, they rely on audiences to engage with their products. In this way, both the media and audiences are able to maintain an element of control in their relationship.

Mark allocation: 3 marks

- 3 marks: The student has constructed a clear and detailed explanation that conveys an insightful understanding of the ways both the media and audiences can exercise agency. Relevant media language is evident in the response.
- 2 marks: The student has provided a general explanation that conveys an accurate understanding of the ways both the media and audiences can excercise agency. Some media language is evident in the response.
- 1 mark: The student has provided a limited explanation of the ways both the media and audiences can exercise agency. Little or no use of media language is evident in the response.

TIP

» **This question asks you to explain and is only worth 3 marks, so your answer may include, but does not require, specific examples.**

Question 16

Sample response

The relationship between audiences and global media institutions such as News Corp has changed significantly over time, and these changes can be seen in the way audiences consume the news. In a more traditional media landscape, audiences had only a limited selection of newspapers, radio stations and television networks from which they could get their news; however, the advent of the internet has shifted this dynamic. In the past, audiences were reliant on the news outlets local to them to provide them with unbiased and accurate reporting, although the biases of particular groups were well acknowledged and a direct result of media ownership. In the modern media landscape, however, the existence of endless sources of news means that audiences can more carefully curate their consumption and seek out media institutions that reflect their needs and values more personally, such as by following accounts like *The Daily Aus* or *The Guardian* on social media platforms.

Mark allocation: 4 marks

- 4 marks: The student has provided an insightful discussion of the way the relationship between audiences and global media institutions has changed over time. A detailed and relevant example has been used to substantiate the response. Effective application of media language is evident in the response.
- 3 marks: The student has provided a competent discussion of the way the relationship between audiences and global media institutions has changed over time. An example has been used to substantiate the response. Appropriate application of media language is evident in the response.
- 2 marks: The student has provided a general discussion of the way the relationship between audiences and global media institutions has changed over time. A limited example may have been used to substantiate the response. Some media language is evident in the response.
- 1 mark: The student has provided a limited or incomplete discussion of the way the relationship between audiences and global media institutions has changed over time. Some part of the question is answered. Little or no use of media language is evident in the response.

Question 17

Sample response

Social media platforms enable users to produce and distribute content in a prolific and instant way, but this has come with significant issues. The ethical issue of the production and distribution of deliberately false information by companies that are able to use paid post content to attract followers has been seen on platforms such as Facebook and Instagram. In July 2021, Meta (then called Facebook) removed 65 Facebook accounts and 243 Instagram accounts from Russia after they were found to be distributing misinformation about the Pfizer and AstraZeneca COVID-19 vaccines. Meta's July 2021 Coordinated Inauthentic Behavior Report revealed the accounts were associated with Fazze, a Russian-linked marketing agency, which launched two campaigns over five months with the aim of spreading untruthful information about the vaccines. These campaigns were primarily targeted at users in Latin America and India at times when their governments were discussing authorisation of the vaccines. Fazze also created Reddit posts suggesting that the AstraZeneca vaccine would turn humans into chimpanzees, and set up anti-vaccine Change.org petitions and shared these with followers. The agency approached a number of social media influencers and offered to pay them to tell their followers that the death rate for the Pfizer vaccine was almost three times the AstraZeneca rate. Ultimately, many of these influencers reported the company to Facebook, which was able to review and remove the content. Despite its efforts, Fazze was largely unsuccessful in reaching a large audience, with only 24 000 followers across the many accounts it created and most posts receiving very little or no interaction from users. However, this example highlights how unethical behaviour can be seen in the production and distribution of media products in the modern media landscape.

Mark allocation: 7 marks

- 6–7 marks: The student has constructed a comprehensive analysis of how a legal or ethical issue can be seen in the production and/or distribution of media products. A specific and detailed example of an issue has been provided. The student has used highly appropriate media language throughout their response.
- 4–5 marks: The student has constructed a clear analysis of how a legal or ethical issue can be seen in the production and/or distribution of media products. A relevant example of an issue has been provided. The student has used appropriate media language throughout their response.
- 2–3 marks: The student has constructed a general discussion of how a legal or ethical issue can be seen in the production and/or distribution of media products. An example of an issue has been provided but may be broad or irrelevant to the question. The student has used some media language throughout their response.
- 1 mark: The student has given a limited or incomplete response that has made some attempt to answer how a legal or ethical issue can be seen in the production and/or distribution of media products. The student has used limited or no media language throughout their response.

TIP

» **Rather than thinking about media products in your response, focus on the companies that produce and distribute media products in order to answer this question effectively.**

Question 18

Sample response

Regulation of the media can be difficult as advances in technology mean regulators have to constantly adapt to new media platforms and their uses. A regulation system that has previously been effective may become redundant very quickly. For example, Netflix has evolved to become a streaming platform that produces its own content, but it was not initially formally regulated. This meant that its content was not necessarily classified by every country that had access to the platform. Australia's government therefore had to work with Netflix to update the way it approached the classification of that content.

Mark allocation: 3 marks

- 3 marks: The student has provided a clear and detailed explanation of why regulation can be challenging. They may have provided a specific and relevant example to support the discussion. Relevant media language is evident in the response.
- 2 marks: The student has provided a general explanation of why regulation can be challenging. They may have provided an example to support the discussion. Some media language is evident in the response.
- 1 mark: The student has provided an incomplete or very limited response that answers some part of the question. Little or no use of media language is evident in the response.

Question 19

Sample response

Modern media users are often connected to digital platforms via smart devices, as seen in the image provided, in which a man clutches a phone in his hand. The collection of user data by media platforms is an ethical issue that is frequently discussed in the modern media landscape. Many media users have at some point expressed concern that their digital movements are tracked and used for ethically questionable purposes; however, some have grown to accept this practice and appreciate the level of personalisation it provides. Others continue to view data aggregation as a breach of their privacy, as indicated by the man in the image looking warily back at the periscope. One example of data misuse is the Cambridge Analytica scandal, in which Cambridge Analytica used the data of Facebook users for political advertising purposes without their knowledge, illustrating the dangers of handing over personal data to web platforms. In response to user concerns sparked by incidents such as this one, Apple developed a privacy feature allowing users to 'Ask App Not to Track' their data, demonstrating an awareness of this concern. However, a study by Lockdown Privacy found that this feature made 'no difference in the total number of active third-party trackers', which has led to accusations that the option gives users a false sense of privacy while their data continues to be tracked. In contrast, media institutions such as Spotify have found ways to repackage data aggregation as a positive component of media use. Spotify Wrapped, which gives users an overview of their yearly listening habits in a social media friendly format each December, has been popular with users, with 1.2 million posts on X (then known as Twitter) referencing 'Wrapped' in December 2019. However, some have still called Spotify's behaviour exploitative, warning that the company stands to gain free advertising from the sharing of Wrapped posts, thus making data aggregation even more beneficial for the company.

Note: This sample response is of a higher level than a typical student response to show the range of detail that can be used to answer this question.

Mark allocation: 7 marks

- 6–7 marks: The student has provided a comprehensive evaluation of a particular ethical or legal issue, with thoughtful consideration of the provided image. The student has discussed the potential harms, as well as the potential benefits, relating to the issue. They have used appropriate examples to support the discussion and demonstrated an insightful understanding of the complexities of the issue. They have referred explicitly and accurately to the production, distribution, consumption or reception of products throughout their discussion, and have used highly appropriate media language throughout their response.
- 4–5 marks: The student has provided a clear evaluation of a particular ethical or legal issue, with consideration of the provided image. The student has discussed the potential harms, as well as the potential benefits, relating to the issue. They have used relevant examples to support the discussion and demonstrated an understanding of the complexities of the issue. They have referred accurately to the production, distribution, consumption or reception of products throughout their discussion, and have used appropriate media language throughout their response.

- 2–3 marks: The student has provided a general discussion of a particular ethical or legal issue, with reference to the provided image. The student has discussed harms and/or benefits relating to the issue. They have referred to the production, distribution, consumption or reception of products, though this may be with some inaccuracies. They have used some media language throughout their response.
- 1 mark: The student has provided an incomplete or very limited response that answers some part of the question. They have used little or no media language in the response.

Note: In addressing the image, students may discuss, but are not limited to, the following: the use of spyware; data aggregation; algorithms; targeted advertising; privacy breaches and hacking; and the prevalence of personal recording equipment in the modern media landscape.

TIP

» **Before you start writing, consider the provided image and jot down some quick dot points noting how it relates to ethical or legal issues concerning media products. Brainstorming these connections before you start writing will make it easier for you to include relevant references to the image in your response.**

Question 20

Sample response

The relationship between the media and its audiences is frequently changing due to technological developments and globalisation. These developments have given audiences the opportunity to become media producers and changed the way media is consumed. Since 2010, audiences have been introduced to platforms such as: Instagram, which encourages users to capture and post photos on a feed; Snapchat, which allows users to communicate via disappearing photos; and TikTok, which asks users to make and share entertaining videos. The role played by audiences has thus changed significantly since the days of analogue media, and it will continue to change as new trends and platforms emerge. For example, BeReal rapidly gained popularity in 2022, and was perceived as more 'authentic' than other social media platforms. Furthermore, the way media is consumed has changed and impacted this relationship. In the days of traditional broadcast media, audiences had fewer ways to access the media in their homes; however, these days, audiences are rarely disconnected. This gives media outlets the opportunity to be more responsive to global trends and situations. For example, in 2021, Disney sent the film *Black Widow* to its streaming platform, Disney+, almost immediately after its release due to the COVID-19 pandemic preventing audiences from attending cinemas. The knowledge that audiences would be more likely to consume the film from home meant the media shifted their distribution methods to fit the audience's circumstances. These changes in media distribution and consumption demonstrate how different generations experience the media differently, due to the dynamic relationship between the media and its audiences.

Mark allocation: 6 marks

- 6 marks: The student has provided a sophisticated analysis of the changing nature of the relationship between the media and audiences. They have used specific, detailed examples that demonstrate the dynamic nature of this relationship and have engaged in a highly appropriate discussion of the factors that have led to these examples. The student has provided a balanced and insightful exploration of both the media and its audience. Effective application of media language is evident in the response.
- 5 marks: The student has provided a detailed analysis of the changing nature of the relationship between the media and audiences. They have used detailed examples that demonstrate the dynamic nature of this relationship and have engaged in an appropriate discussion of the factors that have led to these examples. The student has provided a balanced and considered exploration of both the media and its audience. Effective application of media language is evident in the response.
- 4 marks: The student has provided a clear analysis of the changing nature of the relationship between the media and audiences. They have used examples that demonstrate the dynamic nature of this relationship and have engaged in a clear discussion of the factors that have led to these examples. The student has provided a balanced exploration of both the media and its audience. Appropriate application of media language is evident in the response.
- 3 marks: The student has provided a general discussion of the changing nature of the relationship between the media and audiences. They have used examples to substantiate discussion and shown some understanding of factors that have led to these examples. They have considered both the media and its audience. Some application of media language is evident in the response.
- 2 marks: The student has provided a limited discussion of the changing nature of the relationship between the media and audiences. They may have used broad examples in their response. An attempt to use media language is evident; however, this may be with some inaccuracies.
- 1 mark: The student has provided an incomplete or very limited response that answers some part of the question. Little or no use of media language is evident in the response.

Unit 4 | Area of Study 2 Agency and control in the media Section B

Question 1

Sample response

The relationship between the media and its audience has been frequently scrutinised in an attempt to understand the nature and extent of the influence the media has over its audience, or that audiences have over the media. Early media theories set out to explore the relationship primarily through the lens of the effects tradition, which focused on the effects of the media on an audience. Theories that belonged to this way of thinking, such as the Hypodermic Needle model, considered audiences as passive consumers, receiving messages in exactly the way they were intended, unable to decode the transmission with individuality. However, these beliefs, which suggested the audience were unable to think for themselves, have come to be debunked over time, and are now seen to offer an extremely limited explanation for how media and audiences interact.

Newer theories, such as Eli Pariser's Filter Bubble theory (2011), consider the role of technological advancements and new media developments, acknowledging the capacity of audiences to consume products actively. The Filter Bubble theory suggests that, through their choices and online actions (such as Google searches or engagement with particular pages), audiences become isolated from viewpoints that differ from their own. A recent development relating to this was when Facebook came under fire for its implicit acceptance of companies such as Cambridge Analytica mining and selling internet data to influence election results.

One core belief underpinning new media theories is that audiences are able to exert agency over the media. This can be seen through the impact of fandoms, where the intense scrutiny, analysis and deconstruction of certain media products is given amplified importance due to the shared investment of a community of likeminded people. Fandoms have asserted their ability to resurrect television series that would otherwise have been discontinued, influence story and character arcs through dedicated campaigns and discussions, and bring about more diverse representations through their criticism of casting choices and character construction. For example, the *Veronica Mars* fandom kickstarted the motion picture adaptation of the television series, seven years after the show was cancelled. Furthermore, the content of the film contained frequent moments of fan service, such as the reunion between Veronica, Mac and Wallace, and the revival of LoVe (the fandom shipping name for Logan and Veronica's romantic relationship), both of which serve as examples of how audiences have come to influence the construction of media products.

This increasing agency and the expanding media landscape mean that regulating the media is more challenging than ever. Australia's regulatory bodies no longer have exclusive control over the media, and cannot viably continue to rely on traditional methods of media regulation, such as classification and quotas. Therefore, while audiences are developing power, they are also developing a burden of responsibility. Streaming video-on-demand services, such as Stan and Netflix, are increasingly popular, with the Australian Communications and Media Authority reporting that 66% of Australian adults used online streaming services in 2023. These services require audiences to selectively discern the content that is suited to their needs. This shift of responsibility has, at times, been challenged by unprecedented hurdles, such as the release of Netflix's teen show *13 Reasons Why* in 2017. As an international service, Netflix was able to bypass the regulations in place to protect Australian audiences from harmful content, and the show included a graphic depiction of suicide without providing adequate content warnings or resources to assist viewers with handling the challenging content. As such, schools, parents and the media were required to retroactively debrief the largely teenage viewership in an attempt to help them process what they had seen on the show. Ironically, in an age where audiences are exercising more power, this particular situation reaffirmed the capacity of the media to influence its audiences, with Google noting a 19 per cent increase in searches relating to suicide following the show's release.

The relationship between audiences and the media is deeply complex and transformative, rendering it necessary to continue to revise and reconsider the way it can be monitored.

Mark allocation: 15 marks

- 14–15 marks: The student has provided a detailed and sophisticated response that develops an insightful analysis of how media influence and audience agency have developed or changed. The student has related these changes to issues and challenges relating to regulation and control in a considered and relevant way. The student has used a range of specific, highly pertinent examples to support their ideas, and has employed highly appropriate media language throughout their response.
- 12–13 marks: A detailed and thorough response that develops a well-considered analysis of how media influence and audience agency have developed or changed. The student has strongly related these changes to issues and challenges relating to regulation and control, and has used appropriate, considered examples to support their ideas. They have employed relevant media language throughout their response.
- 9–11 marks: The student has provided a clear and relevant response that develops a sound analysis of how media influence and audience agency have developed or changed. The student has made clear links to issues and challenges relating to regulation and control, and has used appropriate examples to support their ideas. They have employed relevant media language throughout their response.
- 7–8 marks: The student has developed a competent response that develops a general analysis of how media influence and audience agency have developed or changed. The student has related these changes to issues and challenges relating to regulation and control. The student has used relevant examples in their response and has employed relevant media language throughout their response.
- 5–6 marks: The student has provided a general response that develops some analysis of how media influence and audience agency have developed or changed. The student may have attempted to relate these changes to issues and challenges relating to regulation and control, or may have outlined these issues and challenges in brief detail. The student has substantiated their response with a basic example, and has employed relevant media language throughout their response.
- 3–4 marks: The student has provided a basic response that addresses most elements of the question. The student may have used a brief but appropriate example to support their ideas, and employed some appropriate media language throughout their response.

- 1–2 marks: The student has provided a limited or incomplete response that fails to analyse how media influence and audience agency have developed or changed. The response may show some basic understanding of the relationship between media and audiences. The student may have failed to relate these changes to issues and challenges relating to regulation and control, or may have done so superficially. The response may contain limited examples and media language.

TIP

» **This question contains numerous parts that all need to be addressed in your response. Think carefully about how you are going to relate your answer back to each part of the question before you start writing.**

Question 2

Sample response

The relationship between media and audiences has been defined many times by academics and theorists seeking to explain an increasingly complex connection. From the earliest beginnings of mass media to the present digital age, as soon as a theory about influence and dependency has been presented, it has quickly been made redundant by a new development. One of the earliest and most prominent theories, the Hypodermic Needle theory, is a clear reflection of early schools of thought about the media. This theory, which suggests that the media inject their message into a passive audience like a needle, had been used to explain incidents of moral panic, such as the response to Orson Welles' *War of the Worlds* in 1938. The audience's extreme reaction resulted in around one million individuals fleeing their homes or calling the police, reinforcing the idea that the media has a powerful effect on the audience. However, this fails to recognise the other five million who did not respond in such a way. With the development of television and a growing awareness of the role of the audience, the theory was abandoned and is now considered inaccurate.

Theories such as Paul Lazarsfeld's Two-Step Flow theory, coined just a few years after the Hypodermic Needle theory was developed, have had slightly longer periods of relevancy due to their more complex understanding of the relationship between the media and audiences. While the Two-Step Flow theory may be seen as limited in a modern setting due to the restrictive nature of the two steps, it can be loosely applied to some modern media phenomena; for example, the way social media has produced 'influencers', who are paid by companies to promote products to audiences. In 2018, Australian current affairs program *Four Corners* investigated the link between Instagram influencers and the increase in young women seeking procedures such as lip fillers and Botox from plastic surgery clinics, demonstrating that despite its age, Lazarsfeld's theory maintains some relevance.

Similarly, older concepts have been rebranded and reapplied, such as the concept of fandom. Participatory culture has been around for over a century, as seen in the response to Arthur Conan Doyle killing off Sherlock Holmes in 1893, before public outcry forced him to resurrect the detective. Through modern platforms such as X (formerly Twitter) and Tumblr, globalised fan groups are able to unite their voices using Web 2.0 features such as hashtagging to achieve similar goals. One example is fans encouraging Fox to #RenewB99 when sitcom *Brooklyn 99* was cancelled in 2018. Executive producer Mike Schur recognised the audience's active influence in the show's revival, stating 'this happened because fans of the show went berserk', therefore crediting its supporters for what would eventuate into another three seasons for the series. In this way, while the traditional ideas and theories about the complex and interdependent relationship between media and audiences have become less relevant, the core tenets of the relationship are still seen to exist despite the rapidly changing media landscape.

Mark allocation: 15 marks

- 14–15 marks: The student has provided a detailed and sophisticated response that develops an insightful analysis of the changing relationship between the media and audiences, and clearly links these changes to theories of communication. The student has discussed these changes in detail, and has effectively presented different theoretical responses to this relationship from commentators or academics. The student has used a range of specific, highly appropriate examples to support their ideas and has employed highly appropriate media language throughout their response.
- 12–13 marks: The student has provided a detailed and thorough response that develops a well-considered analysis of the changing relationship between the media and audiences, and makes strong links between these changes to theories of communication. The student has discussed these changes in reasonable detail and has presented different theoretical responses to this relationship from traditional commentators or academics. The student has used appropriate and considered examples to support their ideas and has employed relevant media language throughout their response.
- 9–11 marks: The student has provided a clear and relevant response that develops a competent discussion of the changing relationship between the media and audiences, and clearly links these changes to theories of communication. The student has used these changes to evaluate the work of academics and commentators. They have substantiated their ideas with relevant examples and employed relevant media language throughout their response.
- 7–8 marks: The student has provided a competent response that develops a general discussion of the changing relationship between the media and audiences, and links these changes to theories of communication. The student has used these changes to discuss the work of academics and commentators. They have substantiated their ideas with relevant examples and employed media language throughout their response.
- 5–6 marks: The student has provided a general response that develops a discussion of the changing relationship between the media and audiences, and links these changes to theories of communication. The student has attempted to relate these changes to the works of academics and commentators, or may have outlined the key changes in brief detail. The student has substantiated their response with limited examples, and has employed some relevant media language throughout their response.
- 3–4 marks: The student has provided a basic response that addresses some elements of the question. The student has used a brief example to support their ideas and has employed some appropriate media language throughout their response.
- 1–2 marks: The student has provided a limited or incomplete response that fails to develop a discussion of theories of communication. The response may show some basic understanding of the changing relationship between media and audiences. The response may contain limited examples, and limited or no media language is evident.

Question 3

Sample response

Traditional theories about the relationship between the media and its audiences set out to prove that the media had an overwhelming and unilateral influence on audiences. However, this frequently proves to be false in the modern media landscape, where audiences exert influence on the media in equal measure.

The suggestion that the media has the capacity to influence its audience is supported in cause-and-effect cases, which demonstrate the media communicating a message and an audience responding actively. For example, the placement of Reese's Pieces chocolate in the film *ET the Extra-Terrestrial* (Spielberg, 1982) saw a 65 per cent increase in the product's sales. It is believed that in the US, 75 per cent of all broadcast television shows feature product placement, which implies that the positioning of a product in a television show or movie may influence an audience's view of that product.

With new forms of production, distribution, consumption and reception, audiences are also asserting power. One example was the response of Paramount Pictures to audience feedback on the *Sonic the Hedgehog* film, which was scheduled to be released in 2019, but was delayed until the following year in order for the CGI protagonist to be redesigned. Within two days of the film trailer's release, the trailer had more than 20 million views on YouTube, and had received hundreds of thousands of 'dislike' reactions from audiences. In addition, Twitter (now X) was flooded with disapproval, with multiple users criticising the titular character's 'creepy human teeth'. Director Jeff Fowler responded with a tweet that said: 'the message is loud and clear ... you aren't happy with the design and you want changes. It's going to happen.' With the audience having their feedback responded to and actioned, the 'buzz' surrounding the film went from negative to overwhelmingly positive, and this helped the film gain immense popularity. This anecdote reflects the ability of audience members to exert influence through their collective voice and a fast and functional feedback loop.

The extent to which the media and audiences are able to influence one another has more recently become a grey area, with the line between media and audience blurring. The rise of social media platforms has enabled audience members to produce and distribute their own content, which in turn has given way to the concept of 'influencers', as seemingly ordinary users harness their online followings to make money. For example, YouTuber 'Zoella' started out as a teenager vlogging about fashion and beauty from her bedroom in the UK. She now has a net worth greater than US$3.2 million thanks to her 9.9 million subscriber-base, book series and beauty line. The crux of the modern media paradox is represented here – Zoella is a media consumer who has harnessed a media platform to become a media creator, establishing herself as an influential figure to her own audience. Therefore, it is almost impossible to clearly distinguish the extent to which the media and audiences are able to influence one another in the modern landscape, as the roles of media and audience are no longer clearly distinguished.

Mark allocation: 15 marks

- 14–15 marks: The student has provided a detailed and sophisticated response that develops an insightful discussion of how the modern media landscape reflects the agency of both the media and audiences. The student has discussed the extent of this agency in strong detail. The student has used a range of specific, highly appropriate examples to support their ideas and has employed highly appropriate media language throughout their response.
- 12–13 marks: The student has provided a detailed and thorough response that develops a well-considered discussion of how the modern media landscape reflects the agency of both the media and audiences. The student has discussed the extent of this agency in detail. The student has used specific examples to support their analysis, demonstrating a strong understanding of their relevance. The student has used appropriate media language throughout their response.
- 9–11 marks: The student has provided a clear and relevant response that develops a competent discussion of how the modern media landscape reflects the agency of both the media and audiences. The student has thoughtfully referred to the extent to which each party may be able to exert influence and has substantiated this with relevant and specific examples. The student has employed relevant media language throughout their response.
- 7–8 marks: The student has provided a competent response that develops a general discussion of how the modern media landscape reflects the agency of both the media and audiences. The student has used examples to support their ideas and has employed some media language throughout their response.
- 5–6 marks: The student has provided a general response that addresses most elements of the question. They may have focused primarily on either the media or the audience and their capacity to exert agency, rather than considering both. A broad but appropriate example may have been used to support their ideas. The student has employed some media language throughout their response.
- 3–4 marks: The student has provided a basic response that addresses some elements of the question. They may have focused primarily on either the media or the audience and their capacity to exert agency, rather than considering both. The student may have used simplistic examples to support their response. The student has employed minimal use of media language throughout their response.
- 1–2 marks: The student has provided a limited or incomplete response that develops a partial discussion of the agency held by the media and audiences. The response may show some basic understanding of media influence. The student may simply have acknowledged or restated the statement preceding the question. The response may contain limited examples, and limited or no media language is evident.

Question 4

Sample response

An ethical issue that has arisen in the modern media landscape is the perpetuation of misinformation by celebrities on their media platforms. In 2020, the impact of this issue was significant, mostly due to the COVID-19 pandemic and the way in which information about public health was disseminated. In the United States, then president Donald Trump readily distributed his opinions about 'miracle cures' for the virus, such as ingesting disinfectant, and conspiracy theories that suggested the initial outbreak could be traced back to bat soup. Due to the widespread availability of modern technologies and media products, he was able to reach a large and impressionable following, which was seen to have a significant impact on US citizens. This was confirmed through a Cornell University research study that investigated the impact that Trump had by looking into COVID-19 misinformation in the news media, drawing the conclusion that 'the President of the United States was likely the largest driver of the COVID-19 misinformation "infodemic"'. The impact of this misinformation was seen in November of that year, when US COVID-19 infection rates were higher than they had ever been, yet a VoteCast survey showed that almost half of US voters believed the pandemic was under control. Commentators suggested that many of these voters were audiences who had received the message from Trump's televised press conferences and Twitter (now X) feed.

In contrast, an attempt to lessen the impact of COVID-19 misinformation was made through the #passthemic campaign, which saw Hollywood stars hand over their social media platforms to experts in order to promote 'data, facts and science to defeat COVID-19'. Julia Roberts handed over her Instagram account and its 9.2 million followers to then Director of the National Institute of Allergy and Infectious Diseases, Anthony Fauci, who she described in an initial caption as 'the man making sure we get the most accurate, critical information about COVID-19'. He was thus able to distribute a number of Instagram posts containing factual COVID-19 information to her followers.

Furthermore, an interview with Fauci revealed that in April 2020, Kim Kardashian set up a private Zoom call with him and a number of influential celebrities, including Katy Perry, Ashton Kutcher and Gwyneth Paltrow. The call, which was labelled a 'senate of celebrity', was seen by Fauci as an attempt to use celebrity 'megaphones' in order to 'get the word out about staying safe'. This belief in the power of celebrity was also seen when Jerome Adams, then surgeon general of the United States, went on a morning talk show to discuss the virus and stated that 'we need to get Kylie Jenner and social media influencers out there, in helping folks understand that ... this is serious'. The implicit message behind this attempt to gain celebrity support is that when celebrities distribute media products to their audiences, the audiences are likely to receive the message. If this is the case, the impact of misinformation may be strong, but may also be countered by celebrities willing to share legitimate information and facts with their audiences.

Mark allocation: 15 marks

- 14–15 marks: The student has provided a detailed and sophisticated response that thoroughly evaluates the impact that one legal or ethical issue has had within the media landscape. This may relate to the effect of the issue on individuals, governments or globalised media institutions. The student has thoughtfully considered two of the dot points and explained how they are affected by, or contribute to, the chosen issue. The student has used a range of specific, highly appropriate examples to support their ideas and has employed highly appropriate media language throughout their response.
- 12–13 marks: The student has provided a detailed and thorough response that evaluates the impact that one legal or ethical issue has had within the media landscape. This may relate to the effect of the issue on individuals, governments or globalised media institutions. The student has considered two of the dot points and explained how they are affected by, or contribute to, the chosen issue. The student has used specific examples to support their ideas and has employed appropriate media language throughout their response.
- 9–11 marks: The student has provided a clear and relevant response that evaluates the impact that one legal or ethical issue has had within the media landscape. This may relate to the effect of the issue on individuals, governments or globalised media institutions. The student has referenced two of the dot points and related them to the issue meaningfully and has used appropriate, considered examples to support their ideas. They have employed relevant media language throughout their response.
- 7–8 marks: The student has provided a competent response that generally evaluates the impact that one legal or ethical issue has had within the media landscape. This may relate to the effect of the issue on individuals, governments or globalised media institutions. The student has referenced two of the dot points and related them to the issue and has used appropriate examples to support their ideas. They have employed relevant media language throughout their response.
- 5–6 marks: The student has provided a general response that broadly discusses a legal or ethical issue in the media landscape. The student may have referenced only one of the dot points. The student may have used a brief but appropriate example to support their ideas and employed some relevant media language throughout their response.
- 3–4 marks: The student has provided a basic response that refers to a legal or ethical issue in the media landscape. The student may have referenced only one of the dot points. The student may have used a brief example to support their ideas and has attempted to use some media language throughout their response.
- 1–2 marks: The student has provided a limited or incomplete response that may outline a legal or ethical issue in the media landscape. The student may not have referred to any of the dot points or may have done so inaccurately. The response may contain limited examples and media language.

TIP

» **The task word 'evaluate' requires you to assess the issue's impact.**

Question 5

Sample response

In a world where globalised media institutions can reach billions of people in seconds, the regulation and control of content is extremely difficult for national governments to manage effectively.

The rise of streaming services has meant the Australian Government no longer exerts executive power over the content Australian audiences watch on a daily basis; instead, this power is passed to consumers or their parents. This can then lead to reliance on platform features such as separate profiles for children, as seen with Netflix, which are fallible in their attempts to prevent children from watching harmful content. This was evident when an Adelaide principal asked parents of the school community to be vigilant in their efforts to prevent their children from watching Netflix's hit Korean drama, *Squid Game*. The series, which contains dramatic scenes of violence and gore, also inspired a range of TikTok trends, Roblox games and YouTube mashup videos, all of which are potentially accessible to young audiences. For example, on 11 October 2021, Masaka Kids Africana, a YouTube channel dedicated to African children making music videos, released a *Squid Game* inspired 'Red Light, Green Light' dance video, depicting young children acting out getting shot by a machine gun, mimicking a scene in the television show. Despite *Squid Game* receiving a Mature Audience (MA15+) rating, the violent themes were transposed into more accessible forms for children, highlighting the difficulty of protecting young audiences in the modern media landscape.

Another issue with the regulation of the media in Australia is its reliance on self-regulation and codes of conducts that have minor, if any, consequences when the codes are breached. Australia's key regulatory bodies have clear codes of conduct around distinguishable advertising, such as the Australian Association of National Advertisers (AANA) Code of Ethics, which stipulates that advertising and marketing material should be clearly distinguishable with hashtags, identifying them as marketing content for a company. Unfortunately, however, the consequences of a breach are minimal and hardly act as a deterrent. For example, following the release of the Code of Ethics in 2021, influencer Anna Heinrich became the first to be called out for failing to disclose a paid promotion. Heinrich was prompted to add a paid partnership tag to a post, making her collaboration with Runaway The Label transparent to her 300 000 followers. However, despite failing to adhere to the AANA's code, Heinrich received no further punishment for the deceptive practice. Furthermore, by the time she updated the post, it was two months old, an age in social media time, and this move was unlikely to counteract the impact of her initial deception. In the two months following Heinrich's slap on the wrist, at least four other influencers were found to be in breach of the code, reflecting the lack of fear or respect commanded by the AANA and their code. In order for media regulation to be effective, it must be prompt and have meaningful impact, but this is not always possible for Australia's regulatory bodies.

Mark allocation: 15 marks

- 14–15 marks: The student has provided a detailed and sophisticated response that clearly identifies and insightfully analyses two issues or challenges seen in regulation. The student has thoughtfully considered the difficulties faced in regulatory attempts and has used specific, highly appropriate examples to support their ideas. The student has employed highly appropriate media language throughout their response.
- 12–13 marks: The student has provided a detailed and thorough response that clearly identifies and strongly analyses two issues or challenges seen in regulation. The student has considered the difficulties faced in regulatory attempts and has used highly appropriate examples to support their ideas. The student has employed appropriate media language throughout their response.
- 9–11 marks: The student has provided a clear and relevant response that clearly identifies and competently analyses two issues or challenges seen in regulation. The student has appropriately referenced the difficulties faced in regulatory attempts and has used appropriate, considered examples to support their ideas. The student has employed appropriate media language throughout their response.
- 7–8 marks: The student has provided a competent response that identifies and explains two issues or challenges seen in regulation, although one may have been addressed in greater detail than the other. The student has referenced the difficulties faced in regulatory attempts and has substantiated their response with an example. The student has employed relevant media language throughout their response.
- 5–6 marks: The student has provided a general response that identifies and broadly explains at least one issue or challenge seen in regulation. The student has referenced the difficulties facing regulation and may have used a brief but appropriate example to support their ideas. The student has employed some media language throughout their response.
- 3–4 marks: The student has provided a basic response that identifies an issue or challenge seen in regulation, and an example has been used to support the response. The student has attempted to use media language throughout their response.
- 1–2 marks: The student has provided a limited or incomplete response that may outline issues or challenges with regulation and demonstrates some knowledge of regulation in Australia. The response may contain limited examples, and limited or no media language is evident.

Note: Students may be marked at the lower end of each range if they have not discussed each of their selected issues or challenges in equal depth. If students discuss only one issue or challenge, they cannot receive more than 7 marks.

Question 6

Sample response

The modern media landscape has enabled greater scope for both the media and audiences to exert influence. This has come about as a result of changes to the way media is produced, distributed, consumed and received by governments and individuals.

Although there has always existed some form of communication between the media and audiences, the number of pathways through which audiences can provide feedback to the media has risen significantly in the last 20 years and changed this relationship. Initially, providing feedback was slow and labour intensive, often in the form of traditional written letters that took time to respond to. However, the development of the internet and social media platforms has given audiences more agency, evolving their ability to influence the media. In the modern media landscape, audiences can provide feedback faster and more effectively, as seen when Lizzo swiftly changed a lyric from her song 'Grrrls' just three days after its release in response to fans on Twitter (now X) calling out her use of an ableist slur. Tweets were posted tagging the singer, pointing out the slur and how offensive it is and telling Lizzo to 'change the lyric, it's 2022. Do better.' Many of these tweets were circulated on the platform, garnering thousands of favourites and retweets. In addition to changing the lyrics and removing the slur altogether, the pop star posted a thoughtful statement on social media, stating she 'never wants to promote derogatory language', demonstrating the audience's influence over Lizzo's decision to address the language, as well as their capacity to prompt influential figures to publicly speak out against such issues. Many responded positively to Lizzo, not only for taking accountability for her actions and apologising, but also for actioning their feedback in such a quick turnaround. This type of interaction builds an audience's sense of power and highlights ways to engage actively with the media as an individual.

However, traditional media remains influential in modern times. For example, in 2022 the Australian Government announced it was making changes to its regulations on gambling ads in order to better highlight the risks of gambling and discourage Australians from the practice. This change responded to the increasing concern over Australian gambling habits, which more than doubled in the eight years leading to 2020, according to a study led by Central Queensland University. The formerly required tagline on gambling advertising, 'gamble responsibly', was replaced with a rotating roster of lines such as 'You win some. You lose more' to help audiences assess their chance of failure before placing a bet. This move highlights the government's belief in advertising's ability to impact audiences and its intention to influence audiences through counter-messaging. In this way, the influence of both the media and audiences alike can be seen in the modern media landscape.

Mark allocation: 15 marks

- 14–15 marks: The student has provided a sophisticated and detailed analysis of how both the media and its audiences have the capacity to influence in the modern media landscape. They have clearly and insightfully discussed two of the dot points. They have provided specific and highly appropriate examples of how these stakeholders use the media to exert influence. They have discussed specific concepts, such as feedback loops and the use of advertising, within their analysis and have used highly appropriate media language throughout the response.
- 12–13 marks: The student has provided a detailed and thorough analysis of how both the media and its audiences have the capacity to influence in the modern media landscape. They have clearly discussed two of the dot points. They have provided appropriate and specific examples of how these stakeholders use the media to exert influence. They have discussed specific concepts within their analysis and have used appropriate media language throughout the response.
- 9–11 marks: The student has provided a clear and relevant analysis of how both the media and its audiences have the capacity to influence in the modern media landscape. They have discussed two of the dot points. They have provided appropriate and considered examples of how these stakeholders use the media to exert influence. They have discussed relevant concepts within their analysis and have used relevant media language throughout the response.
- 7–8 marks: The student has provided a competent analysis of how both the media and its audiences have the capacity to influence in the modern media landscape. They have discussed two of the dot points; however, one may have been addressed in greater detail than the other. They have provided appropriate and considered examples of how these stakeholders use the media to exert influence. They have referenced relevant concepts within their analysis and have used relevant media language throughout the response.
- 5–6 marks: The student has provided a general discussion of how both the media and its audiences have the capacity to influence in the modern media landscape. They have broadly discussed at least one of the dot points. They have provided appropriate examples of how these stakeholders use the media to exert influence. They have referenced relevant concepts within their analysis and have used some media language throughout the response.
- 3–4 marks: The student has provided a basic response about how both the media and its audiences have the capacity to influence in the modern media landscape. They have broadly discussed at least one of the dot points. They have provided an example to support their discussion and have attempted to use media language throughout the response.
- 1–2 marks: The student has provided a limited or incomplete response that may outline the influence of the media and its audiences. They may not have referred to any of the dot points or may have done so inaccurately. The response may contain limited examples, and limited or no media language is evident.

TIP

» **This question contains numerous parts that all need to be addressed in your response. Before you begin writing, it is worthwhile to jot down a quick plan that sets out how you are going to address each part of the question.**

Extra space for responses

Acknowledgements

Insight Publications thanks the following individuals for their contributions to this resource: Rachael Swatman, Ellie Katsaouni, Anna Muston and Jennifer Varrasso.

Images are from Shutterstock.

Note: Some sample responses were written in previous years and so may include some dated references.